GCSE AQA

English Anthology

Complete Revision and Practice

Covering Poems from Different Cultures

Published by Coordination Group Publications Ltd.

Editors
Harriet Knowles, Katherine Reed, Edward Robinson, David Ryan, Rachel Selway and Jennifer Underwood.

Contributors:
Charley Darbishire, Roland Haynes, Kate Houghton and Elisabeth Sanderson.

With thanks to Paula Barnett and Glenn Rogers for the proofreading.

With thanks to Laura Phillips for the copyright research.

ISBN: 978 1 84762 097 2
Website: www.cgpbooks.co.uk
Printed by Elanders Hindson Ltd, Newcastle upon Tyne.
Clipart source: CorelDRAW®

Contents

ABOUT THIS BOOK

About the Exams

This book is for anyone studying the <u>AQA</u> exam board's <u>Specification A</u> for <u>GCSE English</u>. It's focused on one key part of the syllabus — 'Reading Poetry from Different Cultures.'

You'll have to do <u>2 exam papers</u> for GCSE English and each one is split up into <u>2 sections</u>. The 'Reading Poetry from Different Cultures' exam question is in <u>Paper 2, Section A</u>. This book is designed to help you <u>learn and revise</u> this important part of GCSE English.

The *Exam Papers* are *Broken Down* like this

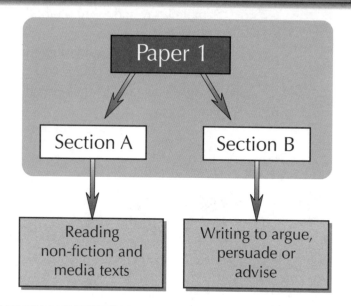

Paper 1

Section A → Reading non-fiction and media texts

Section B → Writing to argue, persuade or advise

You get <u>1 hour 45 minutes</u> for Paper 1.

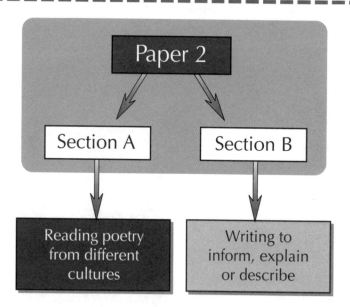

Paper 2

Section A → Reading poetry from different cultures

Section B → Writing to inform, explain or describe

You get <u>1 hour 30 minutes</u> for Paper 2.

Remember that you do <u>both parts of Paper 1</u> in one exam, and <u>both parts of Paper 2</u> in another exam.

So you do the 'Reading Poetry from Different Cultures' section at the <u>same sitting</u> as the 'Writing to Inform, Explain or Describe' section.

This book is focused on helping you with Paper 2, Section A

So there you are, not one but <u>two lovely exams</u> that you have to do to get your English GCSE. Don't worry about Paper 1 for now though — that's for another day. All we're looking at in this book is the first part of Paper 2, but it's good to know where it fits in with the rest of the exams.

How to Use This Book

This book will help you do better in the 'Reading Poetry from Different Cultures' part of the exams. It's full of straightforward ways of getting extra marks. Start by asking your teacher which poems and themes you need to study: some schools get you to study all of them, others just choose some of them.

There are **Four Main Sections** in this book

Section One is all about the **Poems**

There are two pages about each poem. This is what the pages look like:

The poem is on the left-hand page, along with other useful features:

- Important or tricky bits of the poem are highlighted and explained.
- Difficult words are defined in the poem dictionary at the bottom.
- There's a nice picture of the poet and some info about their life.

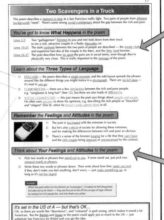

On the right-hand page there are notes about the poem. They talk about:
- What happens in the poem.
- The language the poet uses.
- The feelings of the poet.

There's a bit that will help you to decide what you think of the poem.

There are plenty of practice questions on each of the poems featured in Section One.

Section Two is all about the **Themes**

In the exam, you'll have to compare how two poems relate to one of the themes. There's a page about each of the main themes that might come up in Section Two. The pages tell you which poems use each theme and how different poets treat the same theme. Read it, understand it and learn it. For each theme there are three practice questions to check how confidently you can write about it.

Section Three is all about **Essay Skills** and **Exam Preparation**

Section Three is about the "CGP Five-Step Method" which helps you to write essays that get good marks.

The pages on the left explain the CGP Five-Step Method of answering exam questions.

This method helps you use the information you learn in Sections One and Two to write good essays.

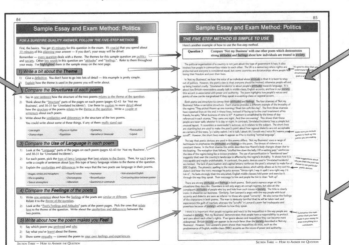

The pages on the right have sample exam essay answers to show you what you're aiming for.

The little boxes at the side are tips on how you can get extra marks in the exam.

Section Four is all about trying some **Practice Exam Questions**

This section contains loads of mock exam questions for you to practise on. You get 45 minutes to answer the 'Poetry from Different Cultures' question in the exam, so practise doing some timed essays.

Edward Kamau Brathwaite

knees spread wide
and the water is hiding

This suggests the low ceilings of the decks of the ship and the limbo dance.

Use of first person engages the reader and makes them sympathetic.

30 limbo
limbo like me

Repetition of these lines emphasises the harshness of conditions on the ship.

One-syllable words and long vowel sounds make this line feel slow and deliberate.

knees spread wide
and the dark ground is under me

down
35 down
down

Before rising out of slavery, he sinks right to the bottom.

and the drummer is calling me

The drum offers hope — it's like a friend to him.

limbo
limbo like me

This line is the turning point of the poem — darkness is replaced by light.

40 sun coming up
and the drummers are praising me

out of the dark
and the dumb gods are raising me

New hope — he's lifted out of the darkness.

References to 'down' and 'up' also create the image of a dance.

up
45 up
up

Here he finally ascends out of the misery of slavery.

and the music is saving me

hot
slow
50 step

The slow three-step beat suggests a weary but steady emergence from slavery, and also the end of the dance.

The full stop at the end — the only one in the poem — represents the end of the dance, of the voyage, and perhaps his life.

on the burning ground.

This fiery image could suggest he's reached hell and that his time in limbo is over.

© Edward Kamau Brathwaite 'Limbo' from *The Arrivants: A New World Trilogy* (OUP, 1973), reprinted by permission of Oxford University Press.

POEM DICTIONARY

Limbo has several meanings —

1. The West Indian dance, crouching backwards to pass under a horizontal stick which some people say originated from the memories of travelling in the cramped decks of the slave ships

2. An imaginary place for the unwanted or forgotten

3. In Christianity, a place where infants who die before baptism go — a place of uncertainty, as they don't know if they're going to heaven or hell

Edward Kamau Brathwaite

Edward Kamau Brathwaite was born in 1930 in Barbados in the West Indies. He's a poet and historian, and he's interested in links between slave nations and their African origins.

Limbo

And limbo stick is the silence in front of me
limbo

limbo
limbo like me
5   *limbo*
limbo like me

long dark night is the silence in front of me
limbo
limbo like me

10   stick hit sound
and the ship like it ready

stick hit sound
and the dark still steady

limbo
15   *limbo like me*

long dark deck and the water surrounding me
long dark deck and the silence is over me

limbo
limbo like me

20   stick is the whip
and the dark deck is slavery

stick is the whip
and the dark deck is slavery

limbo
25   *limbo like me*

drum stick knock
and the darkness is over me

These lines set up the limbo rhythm which is repeated throughout the poem.

The silence is like a threat or a danger sign.

The plodding rhythm of this line adds to the repetitive feel.

The slave ship that took the African slaves to the Caribbean.

This suggests the start of the voyage.

The strong alliteration adds to the impact of the beating of the slaves.

The words "deck" and "dark" are repeated again in lines 21 and 23.

Very similar lines suggest he's completely trapped.

"Stick" has a double meaning — the stick the slaves were beaten with, and the limbo pole.

Darkness symbolises the despair of slavery.

The hard consonant sounds of these words add to the regular, rhythmic feel. These words are also onomatopoeic.

THIS IS A FLAP.
FOLD THIS PAGE OUT.

Limbo

This poem uses the <u>limbo dance</u> as an extended metaphor. The poet uses it to describe the story of <u>African</u> people being transported as <u>human cargo</u> to the Caribbean colonies to work as <u>slaves</u>.

You've got to know *What Happens* in the poem

<u>Lines 1-19</u> The poem begins in the midst of slavery. Two main themes are introduced —
the <u>limbo dance</u>, and the voyage of the <u>slave ship</u>.

<u>Lines 20-36</u> The middle of the poem is the <u>middle of the voyage</u>, right under the stick or limbo pole.

<u>Lines 37-51</u> In the final section, the poet sees an <u>end to the suffering</u>.
He comes "out of the dark" at last — although where he ends up is unclear.

Learn about the *Four Types of Language*

1) <u>REFERENCES TO SLAVERY</u> — this is the main theme. The journey of the first <u>African slaves</u> is linked to the poet's individual life. The <u>past and present</u> are difficult to separate.

2) <u>REPETITION</u> — the lines *"limbo/limbo like me"* are repeated throughout the poem. Some lines are repeated with <u>minor differences</u>, e.g. lines 16 and 17, lines 41 and 43.

3) <u>METAPHORICAL LANGUAGE</u> — descriptions of <u>darkness</u> and the <u>slave ship</u> are used to stress the living hell of slavery. The voyage of the ship is used as a metaphor for the long-term suffering of generations of slaves.

4) <u>RHYTHM</u> — the beat of the <u>drum</u> on the ship emphasises the monotony and relentlessness of slave labour. Also, the tribal beat of the <u>limbo dance</u> recalls the slaves' African roots.

Remember the *Feelings* and *Attitudes* in the poem

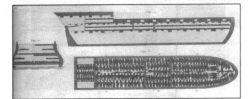

Plan of a slave ship

1) He's <u>angry</u> at the <u>conditions</u> on the cramped slave ship and the <u>cruelty</u> the slaves have suffered (e.g. line 20).

2) But he <u>admires</u> the strength and resolve of the slaves.

3) He <u>celebrates</u> the slaves' past — and their <u>survival</u> (line 47).

> We experience a mixture of emotions in 'Limbo' — we feel the slaves' <u>fear and suffering</u> but also their <u>joy in survival</u>.

Think about *Your Feelings* and *Attitudes* to the poem

1) Pick two words or phrases that <u>stand out to you</u>. If none stand out, just pick two <u>unusual words or phrases</u>.

2) Write these two words or phrases down. Then write about how they <u>make you feel</u>. If they don't make you feel anything, don't worry — just <u>make something up</u>, as long as it's <u>not too stupid</u>.

Example

On line 41 the poet says, "the drummers are praising me". Up to this point, the dance has been symbolic of the monotony of slave life, but it seems to me that the music is now a positive thing. I think the drummers are his African ancestors, helping him out of the hell of slavery.

Talk about the effect of the poem as a whole

The poem is <u>one long sentence</u>. This helps to create the feel of a <u>continuous dance</u>, and the seemingly never-ending suffering of the slaves. Having "and" as the first word suggests this isn't the start of the suffering — it's been going on for <u>generations</u>.

Grace Nichols

© Sheila Geraghty
reprinted by permission
of Penguin Books.

Grace Nichols was born in Guyana in 1950. She was a teacher and journalist in the Caribbean until she moved to Britain in 1977. Both of these cultures and how they interlink are important to her.

Island Man

> The title suggests he's alone.

(for a Caribbean island man in London who still wakes up to the sound of the sea)

> The shortness of the opening line suggests he's jolted awake.

> Compare this with the "grey" London (line 13).

Morning
and island man wakes up
to the sound of blue surf
in his head
5   the steady breaking and wombing

> This line's natural rhythm sounds like the waves of the sea. "Wombing" suggests the comfort and security of his place of birth.

> The natural image contrasts with the "metallic" (line 13) artificiality of London traffic.

wild seabirds
and fishermen pushing out to sea
the sun surfacing defiantly
from the east
10   of his small emerald island
he always comes back   groggily groggily

> The descriptions of his home make it sound like paradise — contrasting sharply with the dreariness of London.

> Could mean "sleepily", or maybe he's been drinking the previous night to try to escape reality.

> The rare use of a capital letter here marks the turning point in the poem.

Comes back to sands
of a grey metallic soar

> This should be "sounds", but he's still tired and thinking of the beach.

> These words can all be applied either to the sea of the Caribbean, or the traffic of London.

to surge of wheels
15   to dull North Circular roar

> The odd placing of this line reflects the man's confused thoughts as he wakes — he's not quite sure where he is yet.

> He has to suppress thoughts of home as he prepares for reality.

muffling muffling
his crumpled pillow waves
island man heaves himself

> This is a nice metaphor. His dreams of the sea comfort him while he sleeps — without them he has to face reality.

Another London day

> This line stands alone to show he's now come out of his dream. The word "another" suggests he goes through this every day.

> Real life is a struggle — both physically and mentally.

POEM DICTIONARY

North Circular — a busy London road

Island Man

In this poem, a man from a Caribbean island is living in London. He wakes up with dreams and thoughts of his <u>homeland</u>, but he's slowly forced to return to the reality of city life.

You've got to know **What Happens** in the poem

Lines 1-10 — The man wakes up thinking of the sights and sounds of a <u>Caribbean beach</u>. But it's an <u>idealised</u> image — he only remembers the <u>good things</u> about it. This seems to show he <u>wishes he was still there</u>.

Lines 11-19 — He slowly "comes back" to the <u>reality</u> of daybreak in London — grey buildings and the sound of <u>traffic</u>. He reluctantly "heaves himself" up to face the day.

Learn about the **Three Types of Language**

1) <u>CONTRASTING DESCRIPTIONS</u> — there are lots of hints that he'd rather be in the <u>natural</u> paradise of the <u>Caribbean</u> than the dull, <u>artificial</u> greyness of <u>London</u>.

2) <u>DREAMY LANGUAGE</u> — some words are strongly linked to ideas of <u>sleeping</u> or waking up. Others have confused <u>double meanings</u>.

3) <u>IRREGULAR STRUCTURE</u> — the line lengths and number of lines in each verse vary, creating a <u>muddled, sleepy feel</u>. Some lines are <u>separated</u> from the rest of the poem and there's virtually <u>no punctuation</u>.

Remember the **Feelings** and **Attitudes** in the poem

1) The poet seems to have <u>empathy</u> for the man, e.g. the description of him "groggily" returning to reality (line 11).

2) There are <u>fond memories</u> of the Caribbean (lines 1-10).

3) There's also a subtle <u>resentment</u> at the London lifestyle and how it intrudes on his dreams (lines 16-18).

4) The poem concludes with a feeling of <u>resignation</u> and <u>dread</u> at the prospect of "Another London day".

Think about **Your Feelings** and **Attitudes** to the poem

1) Pick two words or phrases that <u>stand out to you</u>. If none stand out, just pick two <u>unusual words or phrases</u>.

2) Write these two words or phrases down. Then write about how they <u>make you feel</u>. If they don't make you feel anything, don't worry — just <u>make something up</u>, as long as it's <u>not too stupid</u>.

> **Example**
>
> The line "Another London day" at the end of the poem makes me feel sympathy for the man. To wake up after dreaming about paradise and then realise that you have to face another boring day must be really disheartening. The word "another" suggests he goes through this experience every day.

It's dreamy but it still has a serious point

'Island Man' deals with different cultures in a more easy-going way — it's less cutting than 'Limbo' and 'Nothing's Changed'. But it still revolves around a clash of cultures and a feeling of isolation.

Tatamkhulu Afrika

There's no official segregation, but the feeling of inequality lives on.

25 No sign says it is:
but we know where we belong.

He's an outsider to the luxury of life as a white person.

I press my nose
to the clear panes, know,
before I see them, there will be
30 crushed ice white glass,
linen falls,
the single rose.

Here the glass represents the whites drinking in the splendour of the inn.

The inn and the cafe are close to each other, but completely separate.

Down the road,
working man's cafe sells
35 bunny chows.
Take it with you, eat
it at a plastic table's top,
wipe your fingers on your jeans,
spit a little on the floor:
40 it's in the bone.

The cafe has basic food and plastic tables — compare this to the white people's inn (lines 21-22 and 30-32).

This could mean that black people have lived like this for so long that it now seems natural.

I back from the glass,
boy again,
leaving small mean O
of small, mean mouth.
45 Hands burn
for a stone, a bomb,
to shiver down the glass.
Nothing's changed.

The mark left by his mouth on the glass.

This language shows that the man feels rejected.

"Boy" is a South African word, often insulting, for a black male of any age. It also reminds him that it was the same when he was a child as it is now.

He's angry and wants to take action.

To remove the barrier between black and white.

The poem concludes on a negative note — he doesn't see any difference in post-apartheid South Africa. This makes him very angry.

POEM DICTIONARY

amiable — likeable / friendly
incipient — developing, just starting
Port Jackson trees — large pine trees
haute cuisine — high-class, expensive food
bunny chows — cheap food for the poor

Tatamkhulu Afrika

Tatamkhulu Afrika (1920-2002) was born in Egypt but raised as a white South African. When apartheid was introduced, he refused to be classed as a "superior" white, and moved to District Six in Cape Town. He joined the African National Congress (ANC) and was a political prisoner because of his fight against apartheid.

Apartheid was a system of government used in South Africa, where black and mixed-race people were treated as inferior to white people.

Nothing's Changed

There's a wild and neglected feel to the area.

Small round hard stones click
under my heels,
seeding grasses thrust
bearded seeds
5   into trouser cuffs, cans,
trodden on, crunch
in tall, purple-flowering,
amiable weeds.

Onomatopoeia creates a harsh, bitter mood.

Alliteration and one-syllable words make the tone snappy and hard-hitting.

He prefers the weeds which belong in the area to the splendour of the newly planted trees (line 21) by the hotel.

District Six.
10   No board says it is:
but my feet know,
and my hands,
and the skin about my bones,
and the soft labouring of my lungs,
15   and the hot, white, inwards turning
anger of my eyes.

The recognition is physical.

Suggests he's led a hard life.

The repetition of "and" shows the poet's rising anger.

He can't express his anger and frustration.

Brash with glass,
name flaring like a flag,
it squats
20   in the grass and weeds,
incipient Port Jackson trees:
new, up-market, haute cuisine,
guard at the gatepost,
whites only inn.

The inn stands for the arrogance of the system.

A barrier keeping him out. He can see how the whites live but can't enter.

An ugly word, which suggests the inn doesn't belong there.

This simile shows the proud and insulting dominance of the inn — it seems to be taunting him.

The new inn, with posh food, contrasts sharply with the black people's cafe (34-39).

Presumably there to keep black people out.

THIS IS A FLAP.
FOLD THIS PAGE OUT.

Nothing's Changed

In this poem, the poet goes back to District Six. When he lived there it was a mixed-race area, but when apartheid was introduced in South Africa, it became a "whites only" area. Under Nelson Mandela's government, it was supposedly mixed again — but Afrika sees little difference.

You've got to know What Happens in the poem

Lines 1-16   He describes his return to District Six. He says that, even though the old sign is gone, his senses tell him where he is — "my feet know / and my hands" (lines 11-12).

Lines 17-32   This section's about the inn. The inn represents the reality — blacks and whites still don't mix. It's clear that the inn is for white people only.

Line 33-48   He thinks about the cheap cafe "down the road". It's very different from the inn. In the final four lines, he says he wants to destroy the inn.

Learn about the Three Types of Language

1)   HARSHNESS and BITTERNESS — he's angry at the inequality, and uses harsh-sounding words. They're often one-syllable words, with alliteration and onomatopoeia adding to the harsh feel.

2)   METAPHORICAL LANGUAGE — the glass of the inn becomes a metaphor for apartheid. The inn represents the dominance and arrogance of the white people.

3)   COMPARISONS — the differences between the lives of white and black people give you loads to talk about. Keep an eye out for comparisons split between different verses, e.g. the inn and the cafe.

Remember the Feelings and Attitudes in the poem

1)   There's the physical recognition of the poet's home district (lines 9-16).

2)   But this is tinged with anger at its neglected state, and at the racial inequality that still exists (e.g. line 26).

3)   There's bitterness and resentment in his contrasting descriptions of the white people's inn (lines 17-32) and the black people's cafe (lines 33-40).

4)   This turns to violent feelings at the end of the poem, when he wants to "shiver down the glass" of the whites-only inn (lines 45-47).

Think about Your Feelings and Attitudes to the poem

1)   Pick two words or phrases that stand out to you. If none stand out, just pick two unusual words or phrases.

2)   Write these two words or phrases down. Then write about how they make you feel. If they don't make you feel anything, don't worry — just make something up, as long as it's not too stupid.

> **Example**
> When the poet says, "we know where we belong", it makes me feel angry. Apartheid is supposed to be gone, yet, because of his race, the poet is all too aware of the inequalities that still exist. He's made to feel inferior to white people.

Show you know about the subject

The poet's opinion about South Africa is pretty clear-cut — so you need to go into a bit more detail than just saying, "he reckons it's the same as when apartheid was around". And if you can relate a few points about apartheid or Nelson Mandela to the poem, you'll really impress the examiner.

Imtiaz Dharker

Imtiaz Dharker was born in 1954 in Pakistan. She has said that she believes identity comes from "beliefs and states of mind", rather than nationality or religion.

Blessing

This could refer to the people's dry skin, or to cracks in dry ground.

The skin cracks like a pod.
There never is enough water.

This simple statement sets the scene for what follows.

It's been so long since they've had water, they have to imagine it, rather than remember it.

Imagine the drip of it,
the small splash, echo
5 in a tin mug,
the voice of a kindly god.

Even a tiny amount makes a big impact when there's so little around.

Water is an answer to their prayers.

This extended metaphor shows how valuable water is.

Sometimes, the sudden rush
of fortune. The municipal pipe bursts,
silver crashes to the ground
10 and the flow has found
a roar of tongues. From the huts,
a congregation: every man woman
child for streets around
butts in, with pots,
15 brass, copper, aluminium,
plastic buckets,
frantic hands,

This phrase emphasises both the extent of the rush, and the commotion the water has caused.

This brings to mind a church — they worship the water.

Short lines reflect the frantic rush for water.

The irregular rhyme scheme adds to the bustling feel of the rush for water.

Lack of punctuation creates a breathless effect.

References to brightness and light create a religious feeling — a miracle has happened.

Another religious reference. What many people take for granted is seen here as something to be grateful for.

and naked children
screaming in the liquid sun,
20 their highlights polished to perfection,
flashing light,
as the blessing sings
over their small bones.

Emphasises the life-giving qualities of water.

Alliteration makes this image really stand out.

Goes with the reference to skin in line 1, to create a sense of symmetry.

POEM DICTIONARY

municipal — to do with the city

Blessing

Blessing is set in a massive <u>slum</u> called Dharavi, on the outskirts of Mumbai. The poem describes the reactions of the people who live there to a <u>burst water pipe</u>, and how precious water is to them.

You've got to know **What Happens** in the poem

<u>Lines 1-6</u>   The poet describes the <u>dryness</u> of the slum, caused by <u>drought</u> and <u>no water supply</u>. We get a sense of how every drop of water is <u>cherished</u> by the people living in the slum.

<u>Lines 7-17</u>   A water pipe <u>bursts</u> and loads of people frantically gather round to collect as much water as possible with anything that comes to hand (lines 14-16).

<u>Lines 18-23</u>   The <u>children</u> of the slum are described, basking in the light of the "blessing" (line 22).

Learn about the **Three Types of Language**

1)   <u>METAPHORICAL LANGUAGE</u> — the words used to describe water make it seem <u>valuable</u>. The people of the slum follow it like a <u>religion</u> (line 12).

2)   <u>CHANGING TONE</u> — each verse has a feel of its own. The dreamy <u>fantasy</u> of water in verse 2 gives way to the frenzied pace of the rush when it appears for <u>real</u>. The final verse has a strange, <u>religious</u> feel.

3)   <u>LIFE-RELATED LANGUAGE</u> — the reliance on water for <u>survival</u> is a constant theme.

Remember the **Feelings** and **Attitudes** in the poem

1)   There's a real <u>desperation</u> because of the lack of water — and the poet <u>appeals</u> to the reader to imagine how this would feel.

2)   This desperation leads to the frantic <u>urgency</u> in collecting the water.

3)   There's sheer <u>delight</u> at the rare pleasure of having enough water to drink. The poet uses the <u>sight</u>, <u>sound</u> and <u>feel</u> of water to give the reader an impression of the people's excitement.

Think about **Your Feelings** and **Attitudes** to the poem

1)   Pick two words or phrases that <u>stand out to you</u>. If none stand out, just pick two <u>unusual words or phrases</u>.

2)   Write these two words or phrases down. Then write about how they <u>make you feel</u>. If they don't make you feel anything, don't worry — just <u>make something up</u>, as long as it's <u>not too stupid</u>.

> **Example**
>
> When I read the line "the sudden rush / of fortune", I have mixed feelings. The word "fortune" shows how valuable the water is, which makes me happy for the people of the slum, but it also shows how something that we take for granted seems like a miracle to them. It makes me feel grateful for what I've got.

This poem's not all it seems

It's an odd poem, this one. It's about people living in <u>poverty</u> and desperate to survive, but the tone seems to be quite upbeat — the people of the slum are <u>ecstatic</u> at the sight of water. But that also highlights just how poor they are. So even though it's short, there's lots to talk about in "Blessing".

Practice Questions — *Limbo*

Welcome to the first set of practice questions. There are some warm-up questions to ease you in, then some detailed questions on each of the individual poems. Don't skip this section — it's pretty important stuff.

Warm-Up Questions

1) What is the poem 'Limbo' about?
2) Name one language feature from the poem 'Island Man'.
3) Where is the poem 'Nothing's Changed' set?
4) What event is described in 'Blessing'?

Practice Questions

1   What does the phrase "knees spread wide" tell you about the conditions on the ship?

....

2   Give an example of visual imagery in the poem.

....

....

3   What is the effect of the rhythm of lines 10 and 12?

....

....

4   a)   Why do you think the poet repeats the lines "*limbo / limbo like me*"?

....

....

b)   Find another example of repetition in the poem and describe the effect it has.

....

....

....

5   Pick out a phrase from the poem which stands out to you. Explain why it is significant in the poem.

....

....

....

Practice Questions — *Island Man*

You could skim through this page in a few minutes, but there's no point unless you check over any bits you don't know and make sure you understand everything. It's not quick, but it's the only way.

1   Find two phrases from the poem, one about the Caribbean and one about London, which show their contrasting colours.

Caribbean ....

London ....

2   Which phrase is repeated on different lines to show that the man is gradually returning to reality?

....

3   How does the poet create the effect of being in a dream?

....

....

4   What is the effect of the unusual layout on lines 11 and 14?

....

....

....

....

5   How do you think the man feels at the end of the poem? Give a relevant quote.

....

....

....

6   Now select a phrase from the poem which you can relate to and explain why you chose it.

....

....

....

....

....

Practice Questions — *Nothing's Changed*

Here are some more questions to test your knowledge of the important stuff in 'Nothing's Changed'.

1   What impression do we get of District Six from the descriptions in the first verse?
     What words give you this impression?

     ....

     ....

2   Complete the table below with phrases from the poem which show how the inn and the
     cafe differ.

	The inn	The cafe
Type of food		
Eating surface		
Hygiene/cleanliness		

3   What effect do lines 10 and 25 have?

     ....

     ....

     ....

4   Why does the poet want to act violently at the end of the poem?

     ....

     ....

     ....

     ....

5   Now choose a phrase from the poem which stands out to you. Explain why you like or
     dislike it.

     ....

     ....

     ....

     ....

Practice Questions — *Blessing*

This is the final set of questions for this section. If you don't know some of the answers, just have a quick read through 'Blessing' and the notes again.

1   Write down three words in the poem which create a religious feel.

   i) ....   ii) ....   iii) ....

2   Find a phrase from the poem which suggests:

   a)   a sense of urgency.   ....

   b)   that a miracle has happened.   ....

3   How do you know that water is very precious to the people in the poem?
   Use a quote from the poem in your answer.

   ....

   ....

4   What impression do lines 1-6 give us of everyday life for the people in the poem?
   Support your answer with a relevant quote.

   ....

   ....

   ....

   ....

5   What is the effect of the descriptions of the items the people use to collect the water?

   ....

   ....

   ....

   ....

6   Now you're familiar with the poem, choose a phrase which stands out to you.
   Then explain why you like or dislike it.

   ....

   ....

   ....

   ....

16

Lawrence Ferlinghetti

Lawrence Ferlinghetti was born in New York in 1919. He settled in San Francisco and is interested in how different cultures and races mix. He's concerned about the growing gap between rich and poor.

Two Scavengers in a Truck, Two Beautiful People in a Mercedes

The title reflects the poem's contrasts — the lowly and disgusting scavengers versus the supposedly beautiful rich people.

The whole poem is about this short period of time.

At the stoplight waiting for the light
            nine a.m. downtown San Francisco
        a bright yellow garbage truck
                with two garbagemen in red plastic blazers
5   standing on the back stoop
                    one on each side hanging on
        and looking down into
                    an elegant open Mercedes
                with an elegant couple in it
10 The man
            in a hip three-piece linen suit
                with shoulder-length blond hair & sunglasses
        The young blond woman so casually coifed
                with a short skirt and colored stockings
15   on the way to his architect's office

        And the two scavengers up since four a.m.
                        grungy from their route
                on the way home
        The older of the two with grey iron hair
20   and hunched back
                looking down like some
                        gargoyle Quasimodo
        And the younger of the two
                    also with sunglasses & long hair
25   about the same age as the Mercedes driver

        And both scavengers gazing down
                        as from a great distance
            at the cool couple
        as if they were watching some odorless TV ad
30   in which everything is always possible

        And the very red light for an instant
                holding all four close together
            as if anything at all were possible
                            between them
35   across that small gulf
                in the high seas
                            of this democracy

No movement.

Stark contrasts.

Something in common between the rich and poor.

Repetition adds to the sarcastic tone of this word.

The contradiction suggests this image is false and hypocritical.

The lack of verbs adds to the feel of a still image — nothing is actually happening.

Physically, they look down on the rich people, but only as ugly carved monsters might lurk over good people in church.

The observation is one-way — the rich couple don't pay the binmen any attention.

Another similarity, but only a superficial one.

This could have three meanings — fashionable, unfriendly, and cool in temperature, unlike the hot and sweaty binmen.

It's just a fantasy, and won't affect or touch them in any way.

Emphasises that this won't last or change anything.

It can't actually happen — it's just an illusion.

These two words contradict each other, emphasising that although the gap appears small, it's impossible to cross.

The layout leads to the stress on this last word, where the poet sarcastically refers to the idea of everyone having an equal say.

POEM DICTIONARY

stoop — rear footplate of a truck
coifed — stylishly arranged
Quasimodo — the fictional hunchbacked bell ringer of Notre Dame

hip — fashionable
gargoyle — a carved monster on the wall of a building
odorless — with no smell (American spelling)

Section One — The Poems

Two Scavengers in a Truck, Two Beautiful People in a Mercedes

This poem describes a <u>moment in time</u> at a San Francisco traffic light. Two pairs of people from <u>different backgrounds</u> "meet". There's some strong <u>social commentary</u> about the gap between the rich and poor.

You've got to know **What Happens** in the poem

<u>Lines 1-9</u>   Two "garbagemen" (<u>binmen</u> to you and me) look down from their truck
                 to see a rich, attractive couple in a flashy <u>Mercedes</u> car.
<u>Lines 10-25</u> The stark <u>contrasts</u> between the two pairs of people are described — the <u>trendy clothes</u>
                 and expensive hair-dos of the couple in the Merc, and the <u>dirty</u>, <u>tired</u> binmen.
<u>Lines 26-37</u> The poet describes how <u>far apart</u> the pairs are in social terms, even though they're
                 physically very close. This is really important to the <u>message</u> of the poem.

Learn about the **Three Types of Language**

1)   <u>STILLNESS</u> — the poem describes a <u>single moment</u>, and the odd layout spreads the phrases
     around like the different things you might notice in a <u>photograph</u>. There are <u>no full stops</u> —
     it's read in <u>one go</u>.

2)   <u>COMPARISONS</u> — there are a few <u>similarities</u> between the rich and poor people,
     e.g. "sunglasses & long hair" (line 24), but there are also loads of <u>differences</u>.

3)   <u>SOCIAL COMMENTARY</u> — this just means the poet says things about <u>people and society</u>.
     He often uses <u>sarcasm</u> to show his opinions, e.g. describing the rich people as "beautiful"
     and "elegant" (line 8), when he <u>doesn't really admire them</u> at all.

Remember the **Feelings** and **Attitudes** in the poem

1)   The poet is <u>fascinated</u> with the extremes in society.

2)   But he's also <u>critical</u> of society for allowing these extremes,
     and for making the differences between rich and poor so obvious.

3)   There's a sense of the binmen <u>longing</u> for a life that they <u>can't have</u>
     and the <u>rich couple</u> being <u>unaware</u> or <u>unconcerned</u> by the contrast.

Think about **Your Feelings** and **Attitudes** to the poem

1)   Pick two words or phrases that <u>stand out to you</u>. If none stand out, just pick two
     <u>unusual words or phrases</u>.

2)   Write these two words or phrases down. Then write about how they <u>make you feel</u>.
     If they don't make you feel anything, don't worry — just <u>make something up</u>, as
     long as it's <u>not too stupid</u>.

> **Example**
> When the poet refers to the binmen as "scavengers", it makes me feel disgusted,
> but also sorry for them — they are forced to live off the scraps of hope offered
> by seeing how rich people live, and this feels very unfair.

It's set in the US of A — but that's OK...

OK, so there are words like "downtown", and "coloured" is spelt wrong, which makes it sound a bit
American. But the <u>themes</u> and <u>issues</u> in the poem could apply just as much to the UK — just
substitute San Francisco for Bristol and you get the idea.

Nissim Ezekiel

Nissim Ezekiel was born in Mumbai in 1924, to Jewish parents. But he was raised in a mainly Hindu culture, and has been influenced by atheist views.

Night of the Scorpion

It's from the child's point of view. He's an outsider throughout — he can't affect anything.

He uses a straightforward tone to describe the incident.

These words set the scene by showing it's a poor Indian home.

This simile makes the villagers seem panic-stricken and illogical.

The scorpion is seen as symbolic of the devil.

Again, this shows it's a poor Indian home.

A terrifying image, especially for a child.

They don't seem very bothered about failing to find the scorpion.

The villagers are talking about her reincarnation — they think she'll die.

Sounds like a prayer. But having the same word at the start of so many lines makes this reaction seem repetitive and unthinking. "They said" is also repeated at the end of many lines.

Pain is seen as a way of cleansing the soul before the next life.

There's an ironic feel to this — their reaction has been far from understanding or peaceful.

This shocking sight clearly lives on in the poet's memory, even as an adult.

This shows how desperate the situation is.

All he can do is watch. The adults' actions seem baffling to him.

There's a ceremonial feel to the holy man's actions — they don't seem like a practical solution.

The matter-of-fact tone suggests this was the inevitable outcome — the panic was unnecessary.

He admires his mother for staying calm after all she's been through, and through everyone else's panic.

```
      I remember the night my mother
      was stung by a scorpion. Ten hours
      of steady rain had driven him
      to crawl beneath a sack of rice.
5     Parting with his poison – flash
      of diabolic tail in the dark room –
      he risked the rain again.
      The peasants came like swarms of flies
      and buzzed the name of God a hundred times
10    to paralyse the Evil One.
      With candles and with lanterns
      throwing giant scorpion shadows
      on the mud-baked walls
      they searched for him: he was not found.
15    They clicked their tongues.
      With every movement that the scorpion made
      his poison moved in Mother's blood, they said.
      May he sit still, they said.
      May the sins of your previous birth
20    be burned away tonight, they said.
      May your suffering decrease
      the misfortunes of your next birth, they said.
      May the sum of evil
      balanced in this unreal world
25    against the sum of good
      become diminished by your pain.
      May the poison purify your flesh
      of desire, and your spirit of ambition,
      they said, and they sat around
30    on the floor with my mother in the centre,
      the peace of understanding on each face.
      More candles, more lanterns, more neighbours,
      more insects, and the endless rain.
      My mother twisted through and through,
35    groaning on a mat.
      My father, sceptic, rationalist,
      trying every curse and blessing,
      powder, mixture, herb and hybrid.
      He even poured a little paraffin
40    upon the bitten toe and put a match to it.
      I watched the flame feeding on my mother.
      I watched the holy man perform his rites
      to tame the poison with an incantation.
      After twenty hours
45    it lost its sting.

      My mother only said
      Thank God the scorpion picked on me
      and spared my children.
```

POEM DICTIONARY

diabolic — to do with the devil
diminished — reduced
sceptic — a doubtful person
rationalist — a person who uses logical thinking to explain things
hybrid — a mixture of things
rites — actions in a ceremony
incantation — religious chanting

Night of the Scorpion

The poet remembers a time when he was a child when his <u>mother</u> was <u>stung by a scorpion</u>.
He describes the reactions of various <u>religious people</u> — and seems to think they're all a bit silly.
In the end, his mum <u>survives</u> anyway.

You've got to know **What Happens** in the poem

<u>Lines 1-7</u>   The poet remembers how a <u>scorpion</u>, which had come inside to escape the rain,
<u>stung his mum</u>.

<u>Lines 8-33</u>   Some locals come round and look for the scorpion, but they <u>can't find</u> it
(line 14). They try to help the woman, saying <u>religious stuff</u> about <u>reincarnation</u> —
they clearly think his mum's going to <u>die</u>.

<u>Lines 34-48</u>   His mum's in <u>agony</u> (lines 34-35). His <u>dad</u> does everything he can to <u>cure</u> her.
Then, after all the fuss, she <u>pulls through</u>, and just thanks God it was her and not her
children (lines 47-48).

Learn about the **Three Types of Language**

1)   <u>FACTUAL TONE</u> — there's a neutral, <u>straightforward</u> way of talking when the poet describes
the more action-based parts of the story, e.g. the stinging incident (lines 1-4).
This <u>contrasts</u> with the more ceremonial feel of the <u>religious language</u>.

2)   <u>THE CHILD'S PERSPECTIVE</u> — it's a <u>first-person narrative</u>, so we witness the events through
the <u>child's eyes</u>. He's confused and frightened, as any child would be.

3)   <u>RELIGIOUS LANGUAGE</u> — it's set in a Hindu community, where they believe in <u>reincarnation</u>
— so there's lots of stuff about <u>purifying the soul</u> of sin for the <u>next life</u> (lines 19-28).

Remember the **Feelings** and **Attitudes** in the poem

1)   The poet is <u>frightened</u> by what's happening, but <u>admires</u> his mum's courage.

2)   There's a sense of <u>panic</u> in the villagers' reactions. Even his dad,
who is a <u>rationalist</u>, goes along with the religious stuff (lines 36-40).

3)   The poet seems <u>critical of religion</u> — the ceremonial language and
all that talk of the next life seem <u>unhelpful</u> and premature.

Think about **Your Feelings** and **Attitudes** to the poem

1)   Pick two words or phrases that <u>stand out to you</u>. If none stand out, just pick two
<u>unusual words or phrases</u>.

2)   Write these two words or phrases down. Then write about how they <u>make you feel</u>.
If they don't make you feel anything, don't worry — just <u>make something up</u>, as long
as it's <u>not too stupid</u>.

> **Example**
>
> The phrase "the flame feeding on my mother" makes me feel very uneasy,
> as it sounds like she's being eaten alive. It seems to me that these 'cures'
> are actually making his mother's suffering worse, rather than reducing it.

Compare the last bit to the rest of the poem

The final three lines of the poem are separated from the rest. This last bit's about the mother's calm and
<u>unselfish reaction</u>. It's separate because it's a clear <u>contrast</u> to the <u>panic</u> of the rest of the poem.

Chinua Achebe

This bit links the first section about the vultures to the second section about the commandant.

Evil is personified too, as a persistent reminder of what the Commandant has been doing.

The Commandant is physically unattractive, like the vultures.

He says he's not sure how to look at it — he invites the reader to decide.

The poem concludes on a dark note.

Makes it sound like he's a normal person with a normal job.

The children are described as if they're meat — linking them to the "human roast".

He has a different name when connected with his family — like it's a different version of himself.

Sounds inhuman — like a monster.

Contrasts of size and lightness.

The poet seems to think evil will never go away — it's part of human nature.

30 ... Thus the Commandant at Belsen
Camp going home for
the day with fumes of
human roast clinging
rebelliously to his hairy
35 nostrils will stop
at the wayside sweet-shop
and pick up a chocolate
for his tender offspring
waiting at home for Daddy's
40 return...
　　Praise bounteous
providence if you will
that grants even an ogre
a tiny glow-worm
45 tenderness encapsulated
in icy caverns of a cruel
heart or else despair
for in the very germ
of that kindred love is
50 lodged the perpetuity
of evil.

POEM DICTIONARY

harbinger — a messenger / a sign of things to come
charnel-house — a place where corpses are stored
Commandant — a commanding officer
Belsen — a Nazi concentration camp, where people (mostly Jews) were held and killed during World War II
bounteous providence — the good things that God has given to humankind
encapsulated — enclosed
perpetuity — lasting forever

Chinua Achebe

Chinua Achebe was born in Nigeria in 1930. He worked for the Nigerian Broadcasting Corporation, but when war broke out in 1967, he started to work for the government of Biafra (an area that violently split from the rest of Nigeria). He's written lots of poems about war and its effects.

Vultures

> All these words are related to darkness and misery. They set the tone of the poem.

In the greyness
and drizzle of one despondent
dawn unstirred by harbingers
of sunbreak a vulture

5   perching high on broken
bone of a dead tree

> The vultures live off death.

nestled close to his
mate his smooth

> The vulture's ugliness adds to the evil mood.

bashed-in head, a pebble
10 on a stem rooted in
a dump of gross

> This phrase stands out against the ugliness of the vulture.

feathers, inclined affectionately
to hers. Yesterday they picked
the eyes of a swollen

15 corpse in a water-logged

> Violent image suggests the horror of war.

trench and ate the
things in its bowel. Full

> Nothing is too disgusting for the vultures.

gorged they chose their roost
keeping the hollowed remnant

> They see it as an object rather than something that has been alive.

20 in easy range of cold
telescopic eyes ...
      Strange

> Having this word on its own sounds like he's stopping to ponder on it.

indeed how love in other
ways so particular

> Personification of love.

25 will pick a corner
in that charnel-house

> The idea of love sleeping among corpses is a very bleak image.

tidy it and coil up there, perhaps
even fall asleep – her face
turned to the wall!

> Love ignores evil, instead of triumphing over it — they exist separately.

THIS IS A FLAP.
FOLD THIS PAGE OUT.

Vultures

This poem's pretty grim. We're told how a pair of vultures, despite having some _disgusting_ eating habits, are still capable of _affection_ for each other. The poet compares the vultures to a _Nazi officer_ who's _cruel and murderous_ during the day but _loving and kind_ when he's with his family.

You've got to know **What Happens** in the poem

Lines 1-21   A pair of _vultures_ are described, cuddling up after eating the _eyes_ of dead people.

Lines 22-29   The poet discusses how _odd_ it is that love — seen here as a _person_ —
chooses to _ignore_ the presence of evil.

Lines 30-40   A _Nazi Commandant_ goes home, with the smell of _murder_ clinging to him (lines 32-35).
He buys some _sweets_ for his child waiting for him at home (lines 37-38).

Lines 41-51   The poet finishes by saying you could look at it _two ways_: on the one hand you could be
grateful that such an _evil_ person even has a _shred of decency_ in him (lines 41-47)...
on the other hand, the good inside that person will always be _infected with evil_ (lines 47-51).

Learn about the **Three Types of Language**

1)   CONTEMPLATIVE TONE — although the poet talks about disgusting things, he _doesn't say_
outright that he's appalled by them. He _contemplates_ the evil that humans are capable of, and
how love can't seem to conquer cruelty — he says it's "strange" (line 22), rather than tragic.

2)   EVIL MOOD — the poem starts at dawn, but there's _no sign of the sun_ (lines 3-4). There are
loads of words related to _darkness_, _death_ and _ugliness_ — a solemn mood hangs over the poem.

3)   METAPHORICAL LANGUAGE — the _vultures_ are a metaphor for the evil behaviour of people.
There's a lot of _symbolism_ — love is seen as a _person_, who chooses not to notice the less
pleasant aspects of humanity (lines 22-29).

Remember the **Feelings** and **Attitudes** in the poem

1)   The poet finds the appearance and behaviour of the vultures
(lines 8-21) and the commandant (30-35) _unpleasant_.

2)   But he's _not shocked_ by it. His disgust is detached and _unemotional_
— although this apparent lack of surprise may be intended to _shock_
the reader.

3)   He's _unsure_ about how to look at the fact that people are capable
of both kindness and cruelty (41-51).

Think about **Your Feelings** and **Attitudes** to the poem

1)   Pick two words or phrases that _stand out to you_. If none stand out, just pick two
unusual words or phrases.

2)   Write these two words or phrases down. Then write about how they _make you feel_.
If they don't make you feel anything, don't worry — just _make something up_, as long
as it's _not too stupid_.

> **Example**
>
> The phrase "a tiny glow-worm / tenderness" makes me feel very depressed.
> Although good exists in the Commandant, it seems so insignificant when compared
> to the "icy caverns" of cruelty — it seems impossible that goodness will come out on top.

The link between the vultures and the man is crucial

The stuff about vultures, even though there's a lot of it, is there mainly as a way of _introducing_ the topic of good and evil in _people_, or as a metaphor for the Nazi Commandant. It's as if the poet's seen the vultures feeding, and it's _reminded_ him of the fact that people can do dreadful things. Powerful stuff.

Denise Levertov

Denise Levertov (1923-97) was born in England but moved to New York in 1947. She later became an American citizen, but was strongly opposed to the USA's involvement in the Vietnam War.

What Were They Like?

The poet uses the Vietnamese spelling, rather than the Western version — she sees things from their point of view.

The questions are all in the past tense — this way of life is a thing of the past.

Sounds like a military investigation.

1) Did the people of Viet Nam
   use lanterns of stone?
2) Did they hold ceremonies
   to reverence the opening of buds?
3) Were they inclined to quiet laughter?
4) Did they use bone and ivory,
   jade and silver, for ornament?
5) Had they an epic poem?
6) Did they distinguish between speech and singing?

Shows Vietnamese people's respect for nature, and the simplicity of their lifestyle.

They seem modest and gentle.

Vietnamese is a tonal language — it sounds song-like.

Answers are cautious and vague.

A brutal and bleak way of tracking time.

A poetic but vague way of measuring time.

They lived simple, peaceful lives — this makes the war seem even more barbaric.

1) Sir, their light hearts turned to stone.
   It is not remembered whether in gardens
   stone lanterns illumined pleasant ways.
2) Perhaps they gathered once to delight in blossom,
   but after the children were killed
   there were no more buds
3) Sir, laughter is bitter to the burned mouth.
4) A dream ago, perhaps. Ornament is for joy.
   All the bones were charred.
5) It is not remembered. Remember,
   most were peasants; their life
   was in rice and bamboo.
   When peaceful clouds were reflected in the paddies
   and the water buffalo stepped surely along terraces,
   maybe fathers told their sons old tales.
   When bombs smashed those mirrors
   there was time only to scream.
6) There is an echo yet
   of their speech which was like a song.
   It was reported that their singing resembled
   the flight of moths in moonlight.
   Who can say? It is silent now.

Their hearts have been hardened.

Feels impersonal and unemotional.

The harsh alliteration reinforces the horror of the napalm bombing, which burnt all in its path.

The meaning of bone has changed, from ornamental in the question, to representing the burnt bodies from bombing here.

The paddy fields.

The shocking violence of these two lines shatters the peace of the previous six lines about life before the war.

Sounds like a second-hand account.

The answers conclude with a question — they haven't really answered anything.

Suggests the soft, gentle beauty of their language.

The culture seems lost for ever.

POEM DICTIONARY

reverence — deep respect or worship
illumined — lit up
paddies — waterlogged fields for growing rice

jade — a gemstone, normally green
charred — blackened by fire
terraces — different levels of fields for farming

What Were They Like?

This poem is written as though Vietnamese culture is a thing of the past and someone is trying to find out about it. They ask six questions but the answers reveal that the devastation caused by the war has removed all traces of the culture.

You've got to know *What Happens* in the poem

Verse 1   This is a series of <u>questions</u> about how Vietnamese people used to live before the war. It asks about their <u>way of life</u> (Questions 1 and 4), their <u>culture</u> (Q2 and Q5), their <u>behaviour</u> (Q3) and their <u>language</u> (Q6).

Verse 2   This <u>answers</u> the questions one by one. We're told that they used to be light-hearted and happy, but the war <u>changed</u> that (Answers 1 and 3). Their <u>history is lost</u> and their <u>culture destroyed</u>. The tone of the answers is <u>vague</u> and <u>uncertain</u>, as if the person speaking them can't be sure about life before the war (Answer 6).

Learn about the *Four Types of Language*

1)   <u>RESPECTFUL LANGUAGE</u> — the poet sees the Vietnamese people and culture as <u>beautiful</u> and <u>admirable</u> (e.g. Answer 5). This makes the destruction caused by the war seem even more appalling.

2)   <u>METAPHORICAL LANGUAGE</u> — there's a <u>mythical</u> feel to some of the language (e.g. Answer 5). This is related to the <u>old stories</u> and <u>ceremonies</u> of the Vietnamese culture.

> There's often a <u>mix</u> of <u>formal and metaphorical language</u> in the same sentence. For example, "Sir, their light hearts turned to stone" suggests the person replying might be reporting back on rumours they've heard.

3)   <u>FORMAL TONE</u> — it's based around the style of a formal <u>military investigation</u>. Answers 1 and 3 start with "Sir" — like a soldier reporting back to his superior officer.

4)   <u>SENSE OF DEVASTATION</u> — <u>war</u> and <u>destruction</u> are constant themes. The whole poem is in the past tense, suggesting that everything that's being described has been <u>lost for ever</u>.

Remember the *Feelings* and *Attitudes* in the poem

A paddy field

1)   On the surface of it, the tone is <u>formal</u> and <u>unemotional</u> (e.g. Question 1).

2)   But really the poet is <u>sad</u> about what has happened, and <u>angry</u> at those responsible (Answers 3 and 4). She criticises the <u>thoughtlessness</u> of the war.

3)   There's a sense of <u>regret</u> at what has been lost (Answer 6).

Think about *Your Feelings* and *Attitudes* to the poem

1)   Pick two words or phrases that <u>stand out to you</u>. If none stand out, just pick two <u>unusual words or phrases</u>.

2)   Write these two words or phrases down. Then write about how they <u>make you feel</u>. If they don't make you feel anything, don't worry — just <u>make something up</u>, as long as it's <u>not too stupid</u>.

Example

The phrase, "It is silent now", at the end of the poem, makes me feel desperately sad, because it seems that the war has completely destroyed this beautiful culture.

Match each answer to its question

You might find it useful to tackle the poem by reading one <u>question</u>, then the <u>matching answer</u> — this way, you can see how the use of one word <u>changes</u> between the question and the answer, e.g. "stone" in Q1 and A1. Also, reading up on the background to the <u>Vietnam War</u> will help loads.

Practice Questions — *Two Scavengers*

This is the second set of practice questions. I know it looks dull, but don't miss it out as it'll help you revise.

Warm-Up Questions

1) What event is described in 'Two Scavengers in a Truck'?
2) Who narrates the poem 'Night of the Scorpion'?
3) What does Achebe compare the vultures to?
4) Name one language feature of 'What Were They Like?'

Practice Questions

1   There are loads of contrasts in this poem. Fill in the table below using words from the poem.

	The Scavengers	The Beautiful People
Their job		
Their transport		
Their hair		
Their clothes		

2   Write down three words in the poem which make you think of American culture and language.

   i) .... ii) .... iii) ....

3   Why do you think the poet has chosen not to use any full stops?

   ....

   ....

4   What do you think the poet's attitude towards the beautiful couple in the Mercedes is? Support your answer with a quote from the poem.

   ....

   ....

   ....

   ....

Practice Questions — *Night of the Scorpion*

If you can answer all these questions it shows you've got a pretty good grasp of the poem's main ideas. It's also important to develop your own opinions on each of the poems.

1   Write down a phrase from the poem which shows that:

a)   the poet's mother is in pain.

....

b)   the villagers associate the scorpion with the devil.

....

2   Pick out one idea from the Hindu religion which is mentioned in the poem.

....

....

3   Why do you think the author has chosen to write the poem from the perspective of a child?

....

....

4   What is the effect of the poet describing his father as a "sceptic" (line 36)?

....

....

....

5   What do you think is the poet's attitude towards the neighbours' religious response?
     Support your answer with a quote.

....

....

....

6   Read through the poem again and write down the phrase that stands out the most to you.
     Explain why you like or dislike the phrase.

....

....

....

Practice Questions — *Vultures*

These questions are designed to test how much you can remember from reading through 'Vultures' and the notes — try and complete them without needing to look at the poem again.

1   Fill in the table below with phrases from the poem that describe the different qualities of the vultures and the Commandant.

	The vultures	The Commandant
Ugliness		
Evil		
Kindness		

2   What effect does the phrase "if you will" (line 42) have?

....

....

3   Explain how the poet creates a solemn mood in the poem. Use quotes from the poem in your answer.

....

....

....

....

4   What connection does the poet see between the vultures and the Commandant?

....

....

....

....

5   Pick out a phrase from the poem which stands out to you.
Explain why you like or dislike it.

....

....

....

Practice Questions — *What Were They Like?*

This is the last set of questions in this section of poems — nearly there now.

1   What form does this poem take? Suggest a reason why the author chose this style.

....

....

....

....

....

2   Find a word which has different meanings in different parts of the poem and explain how its meaning changes.

....

....

....

....

3   How is the Vietnamese language described? Use a quote from the poem to back up your answer.

....

....

....

4   What impression does the poem give us of the Vietnamese way of life before the war? Explain your answer with a relevant quote.

....

....

....

5   Read through the poem again and write down the phrase that stands out the most to you. Explain why you like or dislike the phrase.

....

....

....

....

Sujata Bhatt

Sujata Bhatt was born in India in 1956, later lived in the USA and now lives in Germany. She writes in both English and Gujarati, her mother tongue.

from Search For My Tongue

She uses 'I' and 'you' a lot, like in a conversation.

Gets 'you' to imagine what her situation is like. This gets the reader involved.

Repetition strengthens the horrible image.

You ask me what I mean
by saying I have lost my tongue.
I ask you, what would you do
if you had two tongues in your mouth,
5   and lost the first one, the mother tongue,
and could not really know the other,
the foreign tongue.
You could not use them both together
even if you thought that way.
10   And if you lived in a place you had to
speak a foreign tongue,
your mother tongue would rot,
rot and die in your mouth
until you had to spit it out.
15   I thought I spit it out
but overnight while I dream,

મને હતું કે આખ્ખી જીભ આખ્ખી ભાષા,
(munay hutoo kay aakhee jeebh aakhee bhasha)
મેં થૂં કી નાખી છે.
20   (may thoonky nakhi chay)
પરં તુ રાત્રે સ્વપ્નામાં મારી ભાષા પાછી આવે છે.
(parantoo rattray svupnama mari bhasha pachi aavay chay)
ફૂલની જેમ મારી ભાષા મારી જીભ
(foolnee jaim mari bhasha mari jeebh)
25   મોઢામાં ખીલે છે.
(modhama kheelay chay)
ફૂલની જેમ મારી ભાષા મારી જીભ
(fullnee jaim mari bhasha mari jeebh)
મોઢામાં પાકે છે.
30   (modhama pakay chay)
it grows back, a stump of a shoot
grows longer, grows moist, grows strong veins,
it ties the other tongue in knots,
the bud opens, the bud opens in my mouth,
35   it pushes the other tongue aside.
Everytime I think I've forgotten,
I think I've lost the mother tongue,
it blossoms out of my mouth.

Double meaning of "couldn't speak", and "lost my language".

Uses image of two tongues in a mouth to represent speaking two languages.

These words are emphasised by being on a separate line.

Conflict.

Unpleasant image.

Repetition makes the image stronger.

The Gujarati language is spelt out phonetically in English so we can read it and hear the sounds.

Visual contrast to the rest of the poem.

She's still using the image of two tongues competing inside her mouth.

Repeated — for a feeling of wonder and suspense.

A metaphor is used in this part of the poem. The mother tongue is described as if it's a growing plant.

The repetition of 'grows' and the word 'strong' make the mother tongue sound healthy and robust.

She makes the mother tongue sound like a part of nature, with a life and strength of its own.

The plant metaphor is completed with the image of the plant bursting into flower.

POEM DICTIONARY
mother tongue — a person's first language

from Search For My Tongue

This poem is about the <u>conflict</u> between the poet's first language and the foreign language she now uses. The poet is <u>worried</u> she'll <u>forget her first language</u> (mother tongue), but it reappears in her dreams.

You've got to know **What Happens** in the poem

<u>Lines 1-15</u>   Explains the <u>problem</u> she has of being <u>fluent in two languages</u>.
She uses the image of having "two tongues in your mouth" to explain what it is like.

<u>Lines 16-30</u>   When she's asleep she <u>dreams in her mother tongue</u>. This is in the middle of the poem because it's at the centre of the conflict she is experiencing.

<u>Lines 31-38</u>   Describes how her <u>mother tongue grows back</u> every time she thinks she has forgotten it — it is stronger and "pushes the other tongue aside."

Learn about the **Three Types of Language**

1)   <u>CONVERSATIONAL LANGUAGE</u> — in the first part of the poem, the poet uses chatty language (e.g. "I ask you", line 3). It makes it sound like she's <u>talking to the reader</u> about her problem.

2)   <u>FOREIGN LANGUAGE</u> — in the middle part of the poem, there is <u>Gujarati</u> language. This shows us her mother tongue visually, and emphasises its difference from English.

> DOUBLE MEANING
> "Tongue" can mean both the fleshy thing in your mouth and a language.

3)   <u>METAPHORICAL LANGUAGE</u> — in the last part of the poem she uses more poetic language — very different from the chatty language in the first part of the poem. She uses the metaphor of her mother tongue growing back like a flower.

Remember the **Feelings** and **Attitudes** in the poem

1)   She <u>worries</u> that she is <u>forgetting her mother tongue</u> — and that her second language will never feel as natural (lines 1-7).

2)   This is part of a bigger worry that she might <u>lose her Indian identity</u> by living in another country. She's concerned that she's <u>stuck between different cultures</u> (lines 4-9).

3)   She's <u>happy</u> when she realises that her mother tongue will <u>always be a part of her</u> — "it <u>blossoms</u> out of my mouth."

4)   She could be challenging the way English has <u>taken over</u> in many parts of the world, resulting in other languages <u>dying out</u>.

Think about **Your Feelings** and **Attitudes** to the poem

1)   Pick two words or phrases that <u>stand out to you</u>. If none stand out, just pick two <u>unusual words or phrases</u>.

2)   Write these two words or phrases down. Then write about how they <u>make you feel</u>. If they don't make you feel anything, don't worry — just <u>make something up</u>, as long as it's <u>not too stupid</u>.

Example

> On line 38, the poet describes how her mother tongue "blossoms out" of her mouth. I feel this is a particularly powerful image, as it suggests the force of nature is with her when she speaks Gujarati.

This poem is about more than languages...

This poem highlights the difficulties of being part of two cultures — <u>language</u> is an essential part of both <u>culture</u> and <u>identity</u>. There's more about identity on page 52 — other poets focus on this topic too.

Tom Leonard

© Gordon Wright

Tom Leonard was born in Glasgow in 1944. He's often written about people's attitudes to different accents, and says he writes in Scottish dialect so that his 'voice' can be heard through his poetry.

from Unrelated Incidents

> this is thi
> six a clock
> news thi
> man said n
> 5   thi reason
> a talk wia
> BBC accent
> iz coz yi
> widny wahnt
> 10   mi ti talk
> aboot thi
> trooth wia
> voice lik
> wanna yoo
> 15   scruff. if
> a toktaboot
> thi trooth
> lik wanna yoo
> scruff yi
> 20   widny thingk
> it wuz troo.
> jist wanna yoo
> scruff tokn.
> thirza right
> 25   way ti spell
> ana right way
> ti tok it. this
> is me tokn yir
> right way a
> 30   spellin. this
> is ma trooth
> yooz doant no
> thi trooth
> yirsellz cawz
> 35   yi canny talk
> right. this is
> the six a clock
> nyooz. belt up.

The lack of capital letters and speech marks makes it sound informal — like someone's talking. This also shows that the poet won't be forced into using standard English.

Cliché of a posh English accent.

"with a"

"wouldn't want"

The short lines make the poem look like a newsreader's <u>autocue</u>, scrolling quickly down for easy reading. They also add to the <u>abrupt</u>, no-nonsense feel of the dialect.

"commoners"

"talked about"

Says that even people with regional accents don't want to hear the news read in one.

Sounds very disrespectful towards working-class people.

Clearly the newsreader sees regional accents as "the wrong way".

There's an irony in the supposed misspelling of "spelling".

Suggests there are different versions of the truth according to your background.

"you can't"

This defiant way of announcing the news comes across as slightly comical here.

He imitates the newsreader's posh accent in this last bit.

Working-class people are denied the chance to have their voices heard on the news.

from Unrelated Incidents

This poem's about people's attitudes towards <u>accents</u>. The poet imagines a newsreader saying that the news has got to be read in a <u>posh accent</u>, because if it was read in a working-class, regional accent, no one would take it seriously. Confusingly, all this is described in <u>Scottish dialect</u>.

You've got to know **What Happens** in the poem

<u>Lines 1-15</u>	The poet <u>imagines</u> a newsreader saying to him, "I talk with a <u>posh accent</u> because no one wants to hear the news read in a <u>common</u> accent like <u>yours</u>."
<u>Lines 15-23</u>	"If I talked like you, you <u>wouldn't think it was true</u> — you'd think it was just one of you commoners talking."
<u>Lines 24-30</u>	"There's a <u>right way</u> to spell and talk. I'm talking the right way."
<u>Lines 30-38</u>	"This is <u>my</u> truth. You don't know the truth because you <u>can't talk right</u>. Shut up."

Learn about the **Two Types of Language**

1) <u>SCOTTISH ACCENT and DIALECT</u> — the words are spelt <u>phonetically</u>, i.e. they're spelt like they sound. This is vital to the ironic effect of hearing someone with a <u>strong regional accent</u> mocking someone who doesn't like accents.

2) <u>POLITICAL LANGUAGE</u> — accents are linked to <u>class</u>. The poet says that <u>working-class</u> people are <u>denied</u> the chance to use their own voice (lines 32-38). When they listen to the news, it's a <u>posh English</u> person telling them the "trooth".

> **ACCENT AND DIALECT**
> <u>Accent</u> means the way people pronounce certain words.
> <u>Dialect</u> means the words and grammar a person uses, and their accent.

Remember the **Feelings** and **Attitudes** in the poem

1) He's <u>annoyed</u> at the dominance of posh, English accents in the media, and about how working-class, regional accents are not heard.

2) He <u>mocks</u> the idea of snobby people looking down on regional accents as <u>inferior</u> (lines 35-36).

3) He criticises this snobbery in a <u>sarcastic</u> way, by "translating" it into his own dialect.

4) What he's getting at overall is that you <u>shouldn't judge</u> people by the way they talk.

Think about **Your Feelings** and **Attitudes** to the poem

1) Pick two words or phrases that <u>stand out to you</u>. If none stand out, just pick two <u>unusual words or phrases</u>.

2) Write these two words or phrases down. Then write about how they <u>make you feel</u>. If they don't make you feel anything, don't worry — just <u>make something up</u>, as long as it's <u>not too stupid</u>.

> **Example**
> The phrase "wanna yoo scruff" makes me annoyed at the arrogance of the newsreader. He seems to look down on people with regional accents just because of the way they talk.

Think about how the poem sounds when it's spoken
The whole poem is written in <u>dialect</u>, which can make it <u>tricky to understand</u> if you're not used to it. Try to 'hear' it in your head — or even read it out loud. Then imagine your favourite Glaswegian saying it.

John Agard

Explain yuself
wha yu mean
Ah listening to yu wid de keen
half of mih ear
35   Ah lookin at yu wid de keen
half of mih eye
and when I'm introduced to yu
I'm sure you'll understand
why I offer yu half-a-hand
40   an when I sleep at night
I close half-a-eye
consequently when I dream
I dream half-a-dream
an when moon begin to glow
45   I half-caste human being
cast half-a-shadow
but yu must come back tomorrow
wid de whole of yu eye
an de whole of yu ear
50   an de whole of yu mind

an I will tell yu
de other half
of my story

Shows he's willing to hear other points of view.

He's scrutinising you.

He extends the idea of being "half" to the individual parts of his body, to show how silly it is.

Suggests people have made their minds up without even meeting him.

Nonsensical images show how silly the idea of being half of something is.

People have to change their attitudes.

Rhyming makes it seem like a well-planned argument, rather than a rant.

Implies people only see what they want to see.

Suggests the person he's talking to is narrow-minded.

Takes the idea to its extreme — that the poem itself is only half the story.

POEM DICTIONARY

Picasso — the name of a 20th century Spanish painter
Tchaikovsky — the name of a 19th century Russian classical music composer

John Agard

© Sheila Geraghty
reprinted by permission
of Penguin Books.

John Agard was born in Guyana in South America in 1949, to parents of mixed nationality. He came to Britain in 1977. He likes to perform his poems, and believes humour is an effective way of challenging people's opinions.

Half-Caste

Excuse me
standing on one leg
I'm half-caste

> Introduces the subject in a jokey way, poking fun at the term "half-caste".

> Conversational but aggressive tone — this is repeated several times.

5   Explain yuself
wha yu mean
when yu say half-caste
yu mean when picasso
mix red an green
is a half-caste canvas/

> Lack of capital letters could suggest everyone is equal (also on lines 17 and 26).

> He compares having parents of different colour to mixing the colours of a great painting.

10 explain yuself
wha yu mean
when yu say half-caste
yu mean when light an shadow
mix in de sky

> Natural image — shows there's nothing wrong with colours mixing.

15 is a half-caste weather/
well in dat case
england weather
nearly always half-caste
in fact some o dem cloud

> He uses a chatty tone, like he's reasoning with someone in an argument.

> Plays with the double meaning of cast/caste.

> His use of Creole, mixed in with standard English, shows he's comfortable with the different sides to his background.

20 half-caste till dem overcast
so spiteful dem dont want de sun pass
ah rass/
explain yuself
wha yu mean

> Expression of disgust.

25 when yu say half-caste
yu mean tchaikovsky
sit down at dah piano
an mix a black key
wid a white key

> He says we wouldn't have had great music without mixing colours together.

> Piano music uses a mixture of black and white keys, but people don't call it half-caste — so why are people who are part black and part white described like that?

30 is a half-caste symphony/

THIS IS A FLAP.
FOLD THIS PAGE OUT.

Half-Caste

The poet makes fun of the term "half-caste" (someone with parents of different colour). He sees himself as being a <u>mix</u> of things — rather than <u>half</u> of something — and compares it to loads of other things which are great because they're made up of mixtures, like <u>paintings</u> and <u>symphonies</u>.

You've got to know **What Happens** in the poem

<u>Lines 1-30</u>   The poet asks what the term "half-caste" is supposed to <u>mean</u>. He says if you look at things like that, then everything that's <u>mixed</u> could be called half-caste, like great <u>paintings</u> (lines 6-9), the <u>weather</u> (13-15) and <u>classical music</u> (26-30).

<u>Lines 31-53</u>   He <u>challenges</u> people to explain their way of thinking, but finds no logic in it. He <u>mocks</u> the idea by talking about "half" of other things, e.g. line 34. He says people should <u>sort their ideas out</u>, by opening their eyes and their minds.

Learn about the **Three Types of Language**

1)   <u>METAPHORICAL LANGUAGE</u> — he compares being of mixed race to the different colours of a <u>painting</u>, showing it's <u>beautiful</u>, and to the <u>weather</u>, showing it's <u>natural</u>. This is central to his argument against the term "half-caste", which he sees as <u>negative</u> and <u>very insulting</u>.

2)   <u>HUMOUR</u> — he makes the idea of being "half" of something <u>laughable</u>. His humour isn't always light-hearted — his jokes about being half a person are quite <u>scathing</u> (e.g. line 39).

3)   <u>ARGUMENTATIVE TONE</u> — the style is <u>conversational</u> — "yu" and "I" are used a lot — but also <u>confrontational</u>. He challenges assumptions by repeatedly saying "Explain yuself" (lines 4, 10, 23, 31). He uses Caribbean <u>Creole</u> (dialect) and <u>no punctuation</u>, which makes it sound direct and informal.

Remember the **Feelings** and **Attitudes** in the poem

1)   He <u>mocks</u> the idea of mixed-race people being inferior or incomplete ("half").

2)   He's <u>baffled</u> and <u>amused</u> by the idea of being half a person.

3)   He gets <u>angry</u> that people aren't more open-minded, and he <u>tells off</u> these people at the end (lines 47-50).

Think about **Your Feelings** and **Attitudes** to the poem

1)   Pick two words or phrases that <u>stand out to you</u>. If none stand out, just pick two <u>unusual words or phrases</u>.

2)   Write these two words or phrases down. Then write about how they <u>make you feel</u>. If they don't make you feel anything, don't worry — just <u>make something up</u>, as long as it's <u>not too stupid</u>.

> **Example**
> The phrase "half-a-hand" seems funny and absurd. It's a bizarre image, and just shows how ridiculous it is to use the word "half-caste" to describe a person.

The jokes are crucial to the point being made

A good way to pick up marks here is to talk about <u>how</u> the humour helps the poet <u>make his point</u>. It's not good enough just to say a line's funny — you have to <u>interpret</u> what he's actually getting at.

Derek Walcott

*Derek Walcott was born in St Lucia, in the West Indies, in 1930.
His father was English and his mother was African.
He is a poet, playwright and painter.*

Positive prediction.

There's a formal acknowledgement of this "meeting".

Love After Love

The repetition of the word 'will' sounds confident and assured.

Makes the idea of greeting yourself a visual image.

The time will come
When, with elation,
You will greet yourself arriving
At your own door, in your own mirror,
5   And each will smile at the other's welcome,

Short sentences are used for calm, simple instructions.

Suggests returning to something or someone you abandoned.

And say sit here. Eat.
You will love again the stranger who was your self.
Give wine. Give bread. Give back your heart
To itself, to the stranger who has loved you

The self is seen as an abused lover who has remained loyal.

Christian connection — suggests this is a spiritual process.

Suggests that loving another person can be a betrayal of the self.

10   All your life, whom you ignored
For another, who knows you by heart.
Take down the love-letters from the bookshelf

This continues the sentence that starts on line 8.

Another person could never know you as deeply as your self does.

The poet encourages the reader to put the past behind them and move on.

The photographs, the desperate notes,
Peel your own images from the mirror.
15   Sit. Feast on your life.

Suggests removing the false outer layers to reveal the true, inner self.

The only negativity in the poem comes from references to relationships with other people.

Links the theme of eating to the idea that there's loads to celebrate and look forward to.

Love After Love

"Love After Love" is about finding <u>happiness</u> on your own after the end of a relationship. The poet says that being in love can make you forget who you <u>really are</u>.

You've got to know **What Happens** in the poem

<u>Lines 1-5</u>	The poet says confidently that, after splitting up with someone, you'll eventually return to your <u>own identity</u> (lines 3-5) — and you'll be <u>happy</u> about it ("with elation", line 2).
<u>Lines 6-11</u>	There are offerings of <u>food and drink</u> (line 8) — it's a <u>celebration</u>. He says you should get to know your "self" again, as you know yourself better than any other person (line 11).
<u>Lines 12-15</u>	He suggests <u>removing</u> all the signs of previous relationships, like <u>photos</u> (lines 12-13). Just chill out and <u>make the most</u> of your life (line 15).

Learn about the **Three Types of Language**

1) <u>CEREMONIAL LANGUAGE</u> — there are <u>religious</u> references (line 8), and a formal-sounding <u>greeting</u> (line 3). At times it sounds like a religious rite of passage (lines 8 and 15), marking a <u>new start in life</u>.

2) <u>REFERENCES TO THE "SELF"</u> — the "self" is seen as more than just an identity — it's a person <u>within you</u>. The message of the poem is that you <u>neglect</u> this self when you love another person ("whom you ignored", line 10), so you should <u>get to know it</u> again.

3) <u>INSTRUCTIVE LANGUAGE</u> — the style is like a <u>self-help</u> book. It's <u>advice</u> that the poet wants to pass down. There's no 'maybe' or 'possibly' about it — these things <u>will</u> happen (e.g. line 1).

Remember the **Feelings** and **Attitudes** in the poem

1) He's <u>positive</u> and <u>optimistic</u>. He says it's good to have time to get to know yourself again. He thinks you'll be <u>better off</u> this way than you would be living with someone else.

2) There's a <u>calm assurance</u> about the poem. He's <u>reflecting</u> on his own experiences over a long period of time, and he seems <u>confident</u> that what he's saying is good advice.

Think about **Your Feelings** and **Attitudes** to the poem

1) Pick two words or phrases that <u>stand out to you</u>. If none stand out, just pick two <u>unusual words or phrases</u>.

2) Write these two words or phrases down. Then write about how they <u>make you feel</u>. If they don't make you feel anything, don't worry — just <u>make something up</u>, as long as it's <u>not too stupid</u>.

It's OK to be critical like this sometimes — as long as you make sure you explain why you don't like it.

Example

I'm annoyed by the phrase "Give back your heart / To itself". Just because he prefers to be single, he tries to discourage other people from finding happiness with someone else. This attitude seems selfish and defeatist to me.

Exam After Exam

The day will come when, with reluctance, you must face an exam. You will greet your teacher, arriving in the Sports Hall. And your teacher will say, "Sit here. Write your name on the front of the paper. Take pens. Take pencils. Give back all revision materials. Sit. Feast on your exam."

Practice Questions — *Search For My Tongue*

Here's the third set of practice questions. Use the warm-up questions to refresh your memory and then have a go at the others.

Warm-Up Questions

1) Name one language feature of 'Search For My Tongue'.
2) What dialect and accent does the poet use in 'Unrelated Incidents'?
3) Give examples of other mixtures John Agard describes in 'Half Caste'.
4) What is 'Love After Love' about?

Practice Questions

1   What metaphor does the poet use to represent her mother tongue?

    ....

    ....

2   What effect do you think the poet is trying to create by using this metaphor?

    ....

    ....

3   Why do you think the poet uses the words "you" and "I" a lot?

    ....

    ....

    ....

4   In lines 17-30, we 'hear' the Gujarati language. How important do you think this is to the impact of the poem? Explain your answer.

    ....

    ....

    ....

5   Now choose a phrase from the poem which appeals to you and explain why you like or dislike it.

    ....

    ....

    ....

    ....

Practice Questions — *Unrelated Incidents*

These questions will test if you've learnt the main ideas behind each poem — if you get stuck, have a look back at the poem.

1   Which repeated phrase suggests the newsreader looks down on working-class people?

....

2   Rewrite these phrases from the poem into standard English:

      a)   "yi widny thingk it wuz troo"

          ....

      b)   "thirza right way ti spell ana right way ti tok it"

          ....

      c)   "yooz doant no thi trooth yirsellz"

          ....

3   What is meant by the phrase "BBC accent"?

....

4   Why does the newsreader believe that the news shouldn't be read in a regional accent? Support your answer with a quote.

....

....

....

5   Why do you think the poet has chosen to put the newsreader's opinion into Scottish dialect?

....

....

....

6   Choose a phrase from the poem that you find interesting. Explain why you chose it.

....

....

....

....

Practice Questions — *Half-Caste*

Here are some more questions to check your understanding of 'Half-Caste'.

1 Give two examples of natural imagery used in the poem.

1) ....

2) ....

2 At the end of the poem (lines 47-53) what does the poet say people must do before he will tell them "de other half" of his story? Explain what he means in your own words.

....

....

....

....

....

3 How does the poet use humour to make his point? Support your answer with a quote.

....

....

....

....

4 How does the poet create an argumentative tone? Include quotes in your answer.

....

....

....

....

5 Which phrase in the poem stands out to you the most? Explain why you like or dislike it.

....

....

....

....

Practice Questions — *Love After Love*

Finally, here are the last practice questions in this section. Check that you can answer them all.

1   Give two examples of religious / ceremonial language in the poem.

1)   ....

2)   ....

2   Who is the "stranger" that the poet talks about?

....

....

....

3   What advice does the poet give to the reader? Use a quote from the poem in your answer.

....

....

....

4   Why does the poet advise the reader to take down their love-letters and photographs?

....

....

....

5   Does the poet think solitary life is a good or bad thing? Support your answer with a quote.

....

....

....

....

6   Now explain why you like or dislike one phrase which stands out to you in the poem.

....

....

....

....

SECTION ONE — THE POEMS

Imtiaz Dharker

Imtiaz Dharker was born in 1954 in Pakistan. She has said that she believes identity comes from "beliefs and states of mind", rather than nationality or religion.

This Room

This room is breaking out
of itself, cracking through
its own walls
in search of space, light,
5   empty air.

The bed is lifting out of
its nightmares.
From dark corners, chairs
are rising up to crash through clouds.

10 This is the time and place
to be alive:
when the daily furniture of our lives
stirs, when the improbable arrives.
Pots and pans bang together
15 in celebration, clang
past the crowd of garlic, onions, spices,
fly by the ceiling fan.
No one is looking for the door.

In all this excitement
20 I'm wondering where
I've left my feet, and why

my hands are outside, clapping.

It's looking for freedom — breaking away from its usual identity.

Personification of the room.

The bed leaves darkness behind, in favour of enlightenment.

An almost miraculous image.

Dramatic loudness, and again improbable because clouds aren't solid.

Positive, upward movement.

Everyday surroundings seem to come to life and normal routines are disrupted.

It seemed unlikely until the moment it happened.

Food is personified — everything is coming alive.

Even functional objects are now capable of emotion.

More upward movement, to an unlikely height.

They're not looking for a conventional way out.

Related to being grounded. But she's no longer "attached" to them — she's floating.

Now it's specific to her personally.

Hands could represent creativity.

Excitement and congratulation.

Her hands have broken free.

This Room

"This Room" is about a <u>special event</u> in the poet's life, which frees her from the restrictions of everyday existence. She metaphorically <u>rises out</u> of normality and darkness, and into <u>unlikeliness</u> and <u>enlightenment</u>.

You've got to know **What Happens** in the poem

<u>Lines 1-9</u>   The room breaks out of itself, looking for <u>light and freedom</u> (lines 1-5). Then the <u>bed</u> rises into the <u>sky</u> and the <u>chairs</u> follow.

<u>Lines 10-18</u>   The poet says <u>how great it feels</u> when something that seems really <u>unlikely</u> suddenly happens (lines 10-13). <u>Everyday objects</u> like kitchen utensils and food <u>come alive</u> and make loads of noise to celebrate (lines 14-16).

<u>Lines 19-22</u>   It's all been such <u>fun</u> she feels that she's left her <u>feet</u> behind her, and her newly freed <u>hands</u> are applauding her.

Learn about the **Three Types of Language**

1)   <u>PERSONIFICATION</u> — items of <u>furniture</u> come to life (lines 1-9), showing how exciting life has become. Parts of her <u>body</u> become independent (20-22), symbolising her new-found <u>freedom</u>.

2)   <u>IMPROBABILITY</u> — whatever the event is, it clearly seemed very <u>unlikely</u> right until the moment it happened (line 13). This creates the feeling that there's a <u>sudden explosion</u> of happiness.

3)   <u>MOVEMENT</u> — things move <u>upwards</u> (line 9 and 17) and expand <u>outwards</u> (2-3), to show how much <u>richer</u> and full of <u>variety</u> life suddenly is. There's a sense of escaping by being <u>outside</u> her body (21-22).

Remember the **Feelings** and **Attitudes** in the poem

1)   She's <u>excited</u> (line 19) about the special moment in her life when things suddenly change for the better.

2)   She feels <u>joyful</u> and <u>overwhelmed</u> because it's all so sudden and <u>improbable</u> (lines 10-11).

3)   She's <u>relieved</u> that she's finally free (line 22).

Think about **Your Feelings** and **Attitudes** to the poem

1)   Pick two words or phrases that <u>stand out to you</u>. If none stand out, just pick two <u>unusual words or phrases</u>.

2)   Write these two words or phrases down. Then write about how they <u>make you feel</u>. If they don't make you feel anything, don't worry — just <u>make something up</u>, as long as it's <u>not too stupid</u>.

> **Example**
>
> When the poet says, "This is the time and place / to be alive", I'm filled with optimism. It makes me realise that anything is possible, right here and now.

This might seem over-the-top, but examiners want you to sound enthusiastic. So try and stick in something like this occasionally, even if you don't really mean it.

You have to use your imagination

Well, it's nice to have a <u>cheery</u> poem for a change. But what makes this one a bit tricky is that it's <u>not specific</u> about its meaning — it's just generally about some pretty cool stuff going on. So you can be imaginative — think of an <u>event in your life</u> and relate it to the poem. Good times.

Niyi Osundare

Niyi Osundare was born in Nigeria in 1947, and is a Professor of English. He has often spoken out against military regimes in his home country.

Not my Business

He uses first names — it's his friends who are being abused.

This line emphasises the brutality of his beating.

They picked Akanni up one morning
Beat him soft like clay
And stuffed him down the belly
Of a waiting jeep.

The jeep is seen as an animal devouring him.

5   What business of mine is it
So long they don't take the yam
From my savouring mouth?

They violently and noisily disturb the sleeping household.

They came one night
Booted the whole house awake
10 And dragged Danladi out,
Then off to a lengthy absence.

It seems that these are common occurrences.

Using exactly the same words could show that it's an instinctive response — he doesn't want to think about it.

What business of mine is it
So long they don't take the yam
From my savouring mouth?

There's an ironically innocent sound to this — her job hasn't really just disappeared.

15 Chinwe went to work one day
Only to find her job was gone:
No query, no warning, no probe –
Just one neat sack for a stainless record.

Chinwe's treatment isn't violent, but it's still horribly unfair.

They don't have to answer to anyone — they can do what they like.

What business of mine is it
20   So long they don't take the yam
From my savouring mouth?

The simple, factual tone makes it sound inevitable.

Related to the refrain, but now it seems he'll be denied his yam — he's no longer unaffected.

And then one evening
As I sat down to eat my yam
A knock on the door froze my hungry hand.
25 The jeep was waiting on my bewildered lawn
Waiting, waiting in its usual silence.

Use of "the" shows it's the same jeep — so presumably he's in for the same treatment as Akanni.

Menacing, like a predator.

Personification of the lawn stands for the speaker's own frightened confusion.

POEM DICTIONARY

yam — vegetable eaten in hot countries

Not my Business

Another rather bleak one, I'm afraid. From the point of view of an <u>African man</u>, the poet describes how various people in his neighbourhood are <u>mistreated</u>, probably by the secret police or the army. The narrator says that as long as he's left alone, it's <u>none of his business</u>. Then they come for him.

You've got to know *What Happens* in the poem

<u>Lines 1-14</u>	A man called Akanni is <u>beaten up</u> and bundled into a <u>jeep</u> (lines 1-4). Then another man, Danladi, is <u>taken from his house</u> and isn't seen for ages (lines 8-11). After each incident, the narrator says that, as long as he's OK, he's <u>not getting involved</u> (lines 5-7, 12-14).
<u>Lines 15-21</u>	A woman called Chinwe discovers that she's been <u>sacked for no reason</u> (lines 15-18). Again the narrator says that it's <u>no business of his</u> (lines 19-21).
<u>Lines 22-26</u>	As he sits down to eat, he hears a <u>knock on the door</u>. He's really <u>scared</u> (lines 24). He looks outside and sees the jeep <u>waiting for him</u> (25-26).

Learn about the *Two Types of Language*

1) <u>NARRATIVE VOICE</u> — the poet adopts the <u>persona</u> of a passive onlooker who thinks he <u>won't be affected</u> by the violence. This adds to the <u>impact</u> at the end when it <u>does</u> happen to him.

> The last verse doesn't have the usual refrain about not caring — the speaker's voice has been silenced. The poet shows the speaker's attitude is flawed, as no one is safe under this kind of regime.

2) <u>VIOLENT LANGUAGE</u> — the brutality of the regime is shown by comparisons with <u>savage animals</u> (lines 3 and 26). The regime can get away with being <u>openly barbaric</u>, because people are so scared of it.

Remember the *Feelings* and *Attitudes* in the poem

1) The speaker says that what happens to other people <u>isn't his problem</u>.
2) But he's <u>scared</u> when it looks like the same thing will happen to him (line 24).
3) The way the poet describes the abuses (e.g. lines 2 and 17) shows he's actually very <u>angry</u> about them.
4) The message is that you <u>shouldn't ignore</u> these abuses, or one day it'll happen to you too. He thinks people should <u>stand up</u> against oppressive regimes.

Think about *Your Feelings* and *Attitudes* to the poem

1) Pick two words or phrases that <u>stand out to you</u>. If none stand out, just pick two <u>unusual words or phrases</u>.
2) Write these two words or phrases down. Then write about how they <u>make you feel</u>. If they don't make you feel anything, don't worry — just <u>make something up</u>, as long as it's <u>not too stupid</u>.

> **Example**
> The repeated phrase "my savouring mouth" makes me feel angry with the speaker, as he seems greedy and selfish. He turns a blind eye, and seems more interested in eating than in defending his friends.

Think about the poet's reasons for writing the poem

"Not my Business" is a call to people living under brutal regimes to <u>stop ignoring what's happening around them</u>. In your exam, you could write about how <u>effective</u> the poem is, and why.

Moniza Alvi

40 My salwar kameez
        didn't impress the schoolfriend
who sat on my bed, asked to see
        my weekend clothes.
But often I admired the mirror-work,
45   tried to glimpse myself
                in the miniature
glass circles, recall the story
        how the three of us
                sailed to England.
50 Prickly heat had me screaming on the way.
        I ended up in a cot
in my English grandmother's dining-room,
        found myself alone,
                playing with a tin boat.

55 I pictured my birthplace
        from fifties' photographs.
                When I was older
there was conflict, a fractured land
        throbbing through newsprint.
60 Sometimes I saw Lahore –
                my aunts in shaded rooms,
screened from male visitors,
        sorting presents,
                wrapping them in tissue.

65 Or there were beggars, sweeper-girls
        and I was there –
                of no fixed nationality,
staring through fretwork
                at the Shalimar Gardens.

Side annotations:

She likes the Pakistani clothes, but can't feel attached to them. She's also trying to see her identity.

The schoolfriend's reaction to the clothes contrasts with the poet's — so the poet doesn't entirely fit in in England.

The real boat took her away from her homeland.

She must have been very young when she left Pakistan for England.

She can't remember Pakistan properly — she has to imagine it.

This refers to the war when East Pakistan split to become Bangladesh.

The split in Pakistan is compared to her confused identity, split between England and Pakistan.

Her knowledge of Pakistan is based on what she's read and heard.

Brings the poem back to the original theme.

Less positive images of Pakistan.

Sums up her feeling of not being totally English or Pakistani.

There's a barrier stopping her from being part of Pakistan.

POEM DICTIONARY

salwar kameez — Pakistani items of clothing
filigree — delicate gold jewellery
mirror-work — a way of decorating clothing using sequins
Lahore — a city in Pakistan
Shalimar Gardens — peaceful, walled gardens in Lahore

Moniza Alvi

*Moniza Alvi was born in Pakistan in 1954, to a Pakistani father and an English mother.
She moved to England as a child, and revisited Pakistan for the first time in 1993.*

Presents from my Aunts in Pakistan

These words stand out from the English words, just as the presents do from the English clothes she usually wears.

They sent me a salwar kameez
       peacock-blue,
          and another
  glistening like an orange split open,

5 embossed slippers, gold and black
       points curling.

The bright colours of the Pakistani clothes contrast with the clothes she's used to (line 21).

They broke — like her links with Pakistan.

  Candy-striped glass bangles
      snapped, drew blood.
  Like at school, fashions changed
10   in Pakistan —
  the salwar bottoms were broad and stiff,
      then narrow.
  My aunts chose an apple-green sari,
      silver-bordered
15   for my teens.

The presents make her feel out of place in England.

  I tried each satin-silken top —
    was alien in the sitting-room.
  I could never be as lovely
      as those clothes —

She's more comfortable with the plainness of English clothes than the bright colours of the salwar kameez.

20   I longed
  for denim and corduroy.
    My costume clung to me
      and I was aflame,
  I couldn't rise up out of its fire,
25   half-English,
      unlike Aunt Jamila.

Child-like desire for something she can't have.

Refers to the legend of the phoenix rising from the flames — but she can't re-create herself like this.

  I wanted my parents' camel-skin lamp —
    switching it on in my bedroom,
  to consider the cruelty
      and the transformation
30 from camel to shade,
    marvel at the colours
      like stained glass.

The poet feels sorry for the camel whose skin was used to make the lamp. This reflects her own negative feelings about change.

  My mother cherished her jewellery —
35   Indian gold, dangling, filigree.
      But it was stolen from our car.
  The presents were radiant in my wardrobe.
    My aunts requested cardigans
      from Marks and Spencers.

The theft of her mother's jewellery in England could be a metaphor for England stealing her Pakistani identity.

Humorous but regretful — she never wore them.

THIS IS A FLAP.
FOLD THIS PAGE OUT.

Presents from my Aunts in Pakistan

A teenage girl who's grown up in England describes the <u>presents</u> she's received from relatives in Pakistan. Despite thinking the clothes and jewellery are <u>beautiful</u>, she feels <u>uncomfortable</u> wearing them. This makes her think about Pakistan and wonder about her mixed identity.

You've got to know *What Happens* in the poem

<u>Lines 1-26</u>	The poet remembers the <u>clothes</u> her aunts sent her when she was a teenager. When she tried them on, she didn't feel right in them — she thought they were <u>too nice for her</u> (lines 16-20).
<u>Lines 27-43</u>	She thinks of times when the <u>cultures clashed</u>, like the way she felt when her mum's jewellery was <u>stolen</u>, how she <u>never wore</u> the clothes from her aunts, and how her <u>friend</u> didn't like the presents.
<u>Lines 44-69</u>	The poet tries to make sense of the <u>vague memories</u> she has of first coming to England (lines 48-54), and of Pakistan (lines 55-65). She seems to think she'll <u>never feel properly Pakistani or English</u> (line 67).

Learn about the *Three Types of Language*

1) <u>CONFLICT</u> — Pakistan and England seem to <u>contrast</u> in every possible way e.g. the <u>bright colours</u> of the salwar kameez are starkly different from the <u>subdued</u> Western clothes she prefers to wear.

2) <u>PAIN and UNCERTAINTY</u> — her <u>lack of knowledge</u> about the country where she was born (lines 55-59) causes her emotional turmoil. She feels <u>uncomfortable</u> when she tries on the Pakistani clothes (line 17). At the end of the poem, she feels <u>isolated</u> and excluded.

3) <u>METAPHORICAL LANGUAGE</u> — the poet uses metaphors like the <u>situation</u> in Pakistan (line 58) to reflect her own conflict — she too feels "fractured".

Remember the *Feelings* and *Attitudes* in the poem

1) There are memories of feeling <u>confused</u> and <u>out of place</u> as a teenager (lines 16-19).

2) The poet has <u>mixed feelings</u> about the presents and about Pakistan — she finds them <u>attractive</u> and exotic (line 44), but also <u>foreign</u> and strange (line 22).

3) She still feels <u>uncertain of her identity</u> at the end of the poem — she seems to feel like an <u>outsider</u> (lines 67-69).

Think about *Your Feelings* and *Attitudes* to the poem

1) Pick two words or phrases that <u>stand out to you</u>. If none stand out, just pick two <u>unusual words or phrases</u>.

2) Write these two words or phrases down. Then write about how they <u>make you feel</u>. If they don't make you feel anything, don't worry — just <u>make something up</u>, as long as it's <u>not too stupid</u>.

> **Example**
>
> When the poet describes herself as "of no fixed nationality", I feel sorry for her, as I have struggled to work out my own identity. The uncertain tone she has at the end of the poem suggests she is still struggling to resolve her dilemma.

Talk about unresolved conflict

There's a lot you can get out of this poem. Like a lot of the poems, it ends on an <u>uncertain</u> note, so you could write about <u>why</u> you think she's failed to solve her <u>identity crisis</u>.

Grace Nichols

*Grace Nichols was born in Guyana in 1950.
She now lives and writes in Sussex.*

Hurricane Hits England

It took a hurricane, to bring her closer
To the landscape.
Half the night she lay awake,
The howling ship of the wind,
5   Its gathering rage,
Like some dark ancestral spectre.
Fearful and reassuring.

Talk to me Huracan
Talk to me Oya
10   Talk to me Shango
And Hattie,
My sweeping, back-home cousin.

Tell me why you visit
An English coast?
15   What is the meaning
Of old tongues
Reaping havoc
In new places?

The blinding illumination,
20   Even as you short-
Circuit us
Into further darkness?

What is the meaning of trees
Falling heavy as whales
25   Their crusted roots
Their cratered graves?

O why is my heart unchained?

Tropical Oya of the Weather,
I am aligning myself to you,
30   I am following the movement of your winds,
I am riding the mystery of your storm.

Ah, sweet mystery,
Come to break the frozen lake in me,
Shaking the foundations of the very trees within me,
35   Come to let me know
That the earth is the earth is the earth.

Annotations (margin notes):

Suggests she's been feeling alienated from Britain up to this point.

The first verse is the only bit of the poem which isn't in the first person.

The wind is linked to her journey to England.

The personification of the storm here hints at the stuff about the storm gods in the rest of the poem.

She addresses the storm gods in a bold, dramatic way.

Introduces the ancient, historical theme.

The name of a Caribbean hurricane in 1961 — a memory from her childhood.

Caribbean weather is like a family member. It's comforting to her.

Ancient, religious tone.

The lightning could be a metaphor for the enlightenment the storm brings to her.

Just the sight of the storm is awe-inspiring.

Flashes of lightning that caused power cuts.

She's really trying to learn something from what's happening.

Shows the power of the storm, and links it with the sea.

Several possible meanings — could be "Why am I suddenly free from the restraints of England?"

She wants to become one with nature.

Her cultural roots have also been revealed by the storm.

All places on Earth are connected — she no longer feels apart from her homeland.

Hurricane Hits England

In 1987, southern England was hit by a <u>massive storm</u> that caused loads of damage. This makes the poet think of the hurricanes that regularly happen in the <u>Caribbean</u>, and she feels <u>spiritually connected</u> to both the Caribbean and England as a result.

You've got to know **What Happens** in the poem

<u>Lines 1-7</u>	A woman is described lying in bed listening to the <u>raging storm</u>. She finds it both <u>scary and comforting</u> at the same time (line 7).
<u>Lines 8-26</u>	She asks the <u>storm gods</u> why they're visiting England when they usually stick to the Caribbean. She asks why they've uprooted so many massive old <u>trees</u>.
<u>Lines 27-36</u>	She <u>joins together</u> with the gods and feels herself <u>riding along</u> with them. She feels <u>liberated</u> by the experience, and she's <u>less homesick</u> afterwards.

Learn about the **Three Types of Language**

1) <u>HISTORICAL LANGUAGE</u> — the poet uses beliefs from the Yorubas in <u>Africa</u> and the Mayans in <u>Central America</u> about the weather being <u>controlled by gods</u>. Although these gods are scary, she sees them as positive and <u>well-meaning</u>, and talks to them in respectful, <u>dramatic language</u>, e.g. lines 29-31.

2) <u>POWERFUL LANGUAGE</u> — there are lots of metaphors and similes to show how <u>devastating</u> the effects of the storm are, e.g. line 24, where the <u>trees</u> are compared to <u>beached whales</u>.

3) <u>PHILOSOPHICAL LANGUAGE</u> — at the start she feels like she's <u>a long way from home</u>. But the hurricane makes her think about whether it really matters where she lives (line 36).

Remember the **Feelings** and **Attitudes** in the poem

1) At first she's <u>scared</u> by the storm (lines 5-7).

2) Then she makes the connection with the gods, and seems <u>angry</u> with them for coming to England (lines 13-18). There's a tone of <u>indignation</u> in her questions.

3) But then she feels a <u>connection</u> with the storm, and finds <u>meaning</u> in it — she sees it as a <u>link with nature</u> and with the Caribbean.

4) She's <u>grateful</u> to the storm — she thinks it's come to help her (line 33).

Think about **Your Feelings** and **Attitudes** to the poem

1) Pick two words or phrases that <u>stand out to you</u>. If none stand out, just pick two <u>unusual words or phrases</u>.

2) Write these two words or phrases down. Then write about how they <u>make you feel</u>. If they don't make you feel anything, don't worry — just <u>make something up</u>, as long as it's <u>not too stupid</u>.

> **Example**
>
> When the poet refers to the storm as "some dark ancestral spectre", it makes me feel that there's something contradictory about it: the "spectre" sounds menacing, but the word "ancestral" shows that it is linked to her roots, so it could also be seen as comforting.

It's another one about culture and identity

Now this is what I call a poem — loads of <u>dramatic</u> talk about lightning and storm gods, and plenty of cracking <u>metaphors</u> to get stuck into. Just remember it's about more than storms — it shares the <u>cultural theme</u> with several other poems, which you can read more about in Section Two...

Practice Questions — *This Room*

If you've read the notes on *This Room* these questions shouldn't be too hard — remember that the examiner will be looking for your own opinions as well.

Warm-Up Questions

1) Name one language feature of the poem 'This Room'.
2) In which country is 'Not my Business' set?
3) Name one present the author receives in 'Presents from my Aunts in Pakistan'.
4) What effect does the hurricane have on Grace Nichols?

Practice Questions

1   Write down three examples of onomatopoeia from 'This Room'.

  1) ....

  2) ....

  3) ....

2   Write down one example of metaphorical language in the poem and describe what effect it has.

  Metaphor ....

  Effect ....

  ....

  ....

3   How do you think the poet feels about what is happening? Support your answer with a quote.

  ....

  ....

  ....

  ....

4   Choose a phrase from the poem that interests you and explain why you chose it.

  ....

  ....

  ....

  ....

  ....

Practice Questions — *Not My Business*

Make sure you have a good grasp of the images and devices the poet uses and you feel comfortable talking about them.

1   What poetic device does the author use to describe the jeep and the lawn?

....

2   Why is the title of the poem ironic?

....

....

....

3   Why do you think the poet:

    a)   mentions the time of day in the first line of each verse?

        ....

        ....

    b)   describes the victims by their first names?

        ....

        ....

4   What is the effect of the three lines that are repeated?

....

....

....

....

5   Look over the poem again and pick out the phrase that stands out to you most. Explain what effect it has on you.

....

....

....

....

....

Practice Questions — *Presents...*

Make sure you know what ideas and emotions the poet is trying to get across in 'Presents from my Aunts in Pakistan'. These questions will help you form your ideas.

1   Write down three words in the poem which suggest a negative image of Pakistan.

1) .... 2) .... 3) ....

2   Explain what you think the following phrases mean:

a)   "was alien in the sitting-room"

   ....

   ....

   ....

b)   "I admired the mirror-work, tried to glimpse myself in the miniature glass circles"

   ....

   ....

   ....

3   How clear are the poet's memories of Pakistan? Explain your answer.

   ....

   ....

   ....

4   How does the poet feel about her identity at the end of the poem?
     Support your answer with a quote.

   ....

   ....

   ....

5   Write down a phrase from the poem that grabs your attention.
     Briefly explain why you like or dislike it.

   ....

   ....

   ....

   ....

Practice Questions — *Hurricane Hits England*

This is the last set of questions in Section One. If you can complete these you might be ready to move on to revising themes.

1   In your own words, write a summary of what happens in the poem.

....

....

....

....

2   What real-life event is the poem based on?

....

3   What are Oya, Huracan and Shango?

....

....

4   How has the character in the poem been feeling before the storm?
    Use a quotation in your answer.

....

....

....

....

5   What do you think the last line of the poem means?

....

....

....

6   For one last time — choose a phrase that stands out to you in the poem and explain
    why you like or dislike it.

....

....

....

....

Identity

Identity in these poems is about who we are and what has made us like this.

1) It's about being young or old, male or female, rich or poor, powerful or weak, victim or tyrant, confident or uncertain.

2) It's also about where you come from. Which country, region, background and political system you're from.

3) Other aspects also determine your identity — your language, your family, your customs, your ethnicity, your religion, your history and past experiences. They're all part of what makes each of us individual.

Identity is what we Think of Ourselves

Search For My Tongue (Pages 28-29)

1) The poet is fluent in two languages, but the English, "foreign", tongue dominates.
2) She's worried that she has lost her mother tongue, which she feels is part of her identity.
3) She's relieved when she realises that her mother tongue, Gujarati, is strong and will always be there.

Hurricane Hits England (Pages 46-47)

1) The storm awakens the poet from her "frozen" state.
2) She has settled in England but does not feel completely at home.
3) The violence of the storm reminds her of her home in the Caribbean, and her ancestral roots in Africa.
4) She regains her sense of identity, and makes connections between England and her homeland. She realises that the Earth is a whole, and that we should never feel cut off from our roots.

Presents from my Aunts in Pakistan (Pages 44-45)

1) The teenager is confused about her identity as she is split between being Pakistani and being English.
2) All the exotic clothes sent by her aunts attract her, but they also embarrass her.
3) She doesn't decide where she belongs by the end of the poem.

Identity is also what Others Think of Us

Nothing's Changed (Pages 8-9)

1) This poem traces the anger of a South African man when he returns to the area where he used to live.
2) Although apartheid has been abolished, inequalities between different races remain.
3) So the poet's identity is partly imposed on him by other people — he's treated as a second-class citizen because of his race.

Unrelated Incidents (Pages 30-31)

1) The poet is angry that his Glaswegian dialect is not taken seriously or trusted in society.
2) The poem shows us that we'd be shocked to hear the news read in this way — we're used to a posh accent telling us the "truth" of the news.
3) So the poem shows us that dialect can be part of identity, because society sometimes judges people by the way they speak.

The poet's sense of identity puts the poem in context

'Love After Love' (pages 34-35), 'This Room' (40-41), and 'Limbo' (4-5) also talk about identity. In some poems, like 'Presents from my Aunts in Pakistan', it's the poet's main reason for writing. It's important to understand the poet's sense of identity, as it can explain why they feel like they do.

Practice Questions — *Identity*

These questions are about how well you can write about identity as a theme — make sure you can write confidently about identity in a couple of the poems below.

These Poems are about Identity:

Limbo (pages 4-5)
Island Man (pages 6-7)
Nothing's Changed (pages 8-9)
Search For My Tongue (pages 28-29)
Unrelated Incidents (pages 30-31)

Half-Caste (pages 32-33)
Love After Love (pages 34-35)
This Room (pages 40-41)
Presents from my Aunts in Pakistan (pages 44-45)
Hurricane Hits England (pages 46-47)

1   Write a couple of sentences about your identity.

....

....

....

....

....

2   Choose a poem that you know from the top of the page.
    What does this poem say about the way people think of themselves?

....

....

....

....

....

3   Pick another poem that you know from the list at the top of the page.
    What does this poem say about how people view others?

....

....

....

....

....

Political Dimension

Politics means how a country is run, and how a government treats its citizens.
Politics affects both society as a whole and individual people.

> 1) Politics can be about the differences between rich and poor.
> 2) It can be about how leaders use and abuse their power.
> 3) Politics can be about certain groups gaining power and oppressing other groups.

Politics is about Inequality

Nothing's Changed (Pages 8-9)

1) It's set in Nelson Mandela's new South African democracy — apartheid has been officially abolished.
2) But the poet finds that there are still inequalities — the "whites only inn" is still closed to non-whites even though it no longer says so, so he goes to the grimy "working man's cafe".
3) There are two kinds of inequality here — the quality of life you have, and what race you are.

Two Scavengers in a Truck... (Pages 16-17)

1) The gap between the rich and poor is very clear.
2) The USA prides itself on equal opportunity for all — but here we're shown the "gulf" that exists between the "casually coifed" young woman and the "grungy" garbage men.
3) The poet condemns this failure in the political system.

Vultures (Pages 20-21)

1) The Commandant represents Nazi Germany's abuse of power — the Nazis murdered millions of Jews because they believed in the racial superiority of white, "Aryan" people.
2) This destruction of another culture and race was government policy.

It's also about people's Attitudes and Opinions

What Were They Like? (Pages 22-23)

1) Many people were against America's involvement in the Vietnam War in the 1960s and 1970s.
2) The poet shows her opposition to the war by describing an extreme vision of the future, where all Vietnamese culture has been wiped out by the shock and violence of the war.

Unrelated Incidents (Pages 30-31)

1) "Unrelated Incidents" is about the power that language holds. The poet says a Glaswegian accent delivering the news would not be believed or respected.
2) The political dimension here involves us all and the judgements we make about people because of how they speak. Certain accents are associated with authority; others are treated as inferior.

You don't have to be Jeremy Paxman

Don't panic if your knowledge of world politics is a bit scratchy. It can help to know the odd fact, but you can work a lot out just from the poems — so don't go thinking you have to know the complete socio-political history of Nigeria. It's an English exam, not Politics.

Practice Questions — *Political Dimension*

If you understand the themes it'll help you understand the poems — but don't get carried away talking about politics and society and forget to talk about the poem in the exam.

These Poems are about Politics:

Nothing's Changed (pages 8-9)
Two Scavengers in a Truck... (pages 16-17)
Vultures (pages 20-21)

What Were They Like? (pages 22-23)
Unrelated Incidents (pages 30-31)
Not my Business (pages 42-44)

1   If you were to write a poem about a political issue, which issue would you choose, and why?

....

....

....

....

....

....

2   Choose a poem from the top of the page that you know well.
     What political situation does the poet describe, and what is his or her attitude towards it?

....

....

....

....

....

....

3   Choose a different poem. What is the poet's political viewpoint in this poem?

....

....

....

....

....

....

Change

Some of the poems deal with a <u>change</u> in the poet's life, or in the world. This can be a change of <u>circumstance</u> or a change in <u>personality</u>, and it can be positive or negative.

1) People can experience a change which <u>frees them</u> from their problems.

2) Things can change for the <u>worse</u> — on a temporary or permanent basis.

3) Things may <u>appear</u> to have changed but in fact be very <u>similar</u> to how they always were.

Things can change for the *Better*

Search For My Tongue *(Pages 28-29)*

1) The poet is worried that she's <u>lost her mother tongue</u> (Gujarati) because her "foreign" tongue (English) has taken over.

2) A <u>positive change</u> occurs when she dreams in Gujarati and realises it will <u>always be with her</u>.

3) This change is <u>internal</u> and <u>personal</u>.

This Room *(Pages 40-41)*

1) This poem is about a <u>sudden and unexpected change</u> in the poet's life.

2) We <u>don't know exactly</u> what this change is.

3) But it's clearly a <u>positive</u> one, that will affect her life in a <u>massive</u> way — "This is the time and place / to be alive".

Change can also be a *Bad Thing*

What Were They Like? *(Pages 22-23)*

1) The poet describes a <u>negative change</u> — the traditional Vietnamese culture has been <u>destroyed</u>.

2) It seems like this is a <u>permanent loss</u>. The poem concludes with "It is silent now".

Presents from my Aunts in Pakistan *(Pages 44-45)*

1) In this poem, the poet is <u>afraid of change</u> — trying to wear clothes she's not used to wearing makes her <u>uncomfortable</u>.

2) This causes her way of <u>thinking about herself</u> to change. She now has to confront <u>both sides</u> of her background, whereas before she had <u>ignored</u> her Pakistani roots.

3) She also mentions a <u>change in the past</u>, i.e. when she first came to England from Pakistan as a small child. This change is what has <u>led to the current situation</u>.

Nothing's Changed *(Pages 8-9)*

1) In between the poet's last visit to District Six and the visit he describes in the poem, there's been a major <u>political change</u> — apartheid has been abolished.

2) In theory, this is a <u>positive</u> change, as all races are now <u>officially equal</u>.

3) But, in terms of <u>attitudes</u> and the <u>way people live</u>, the poet says that things <u>haven't changed</u> at all — non-white people are still treated as inferior.

Some poets call for change, others criticise it

It's a fairly open topic, so there are loads of <u>angles</u> you could tackle it from. The changes described in any two of the poems on this page will have things <u>in common</u> and things that are <u>different</u>.

Practice Questions — *Change*

Many of the poets in the anthology write about a significant change in their lives — make sure you understand what the change is and how it affects the poet.

These Poems are about Change:

Nothing's Changed (pages 8-9)
Blessing (pages 10-11)
What Were They Like? (pages 22-23)
Search For My Tongue (pages 28-29)

Love After Love (pages 34-35)
This Room (pages 40-41)
Presents from my Aunts in Pakistan (pages 44-45)
Hurricane Hits England (pages 46-47)

1   Write a couple of sentences about a change that has happened in your life.

   ....

   ....

   ....

   ....

   ....

   ....

2   Choose a poem that you know from the top of the page.
    What kind of change does this poem describe?

   ....

   ....

   ....

   ....

   ....

3   Choose a different poem. Does the poet see change as a positive or a negative thing? Why?

   ....

   ....

   ....

   ....

   ....

People

The poems talk about the lives of both <u>individuals</u> and <u>groups</u> of people.

1) Some poets are interested in <u>society</u>, and people's attitudes towards (and treatment of) each other.
2) Sometimes one <u>group</u> of people live a completely <u>different lifestyle</u> from that of another group.
3) Others are interested in people who are <u>on their own</u>, and get on with things as <u>individuals</u>.

*People are **Affected by Society***

Half-Caste (Pages 32-33)

1) The <u>words</u> people use can show the <u>attitudes</u> they have towards different groups in society.
2) The poet says the term "half-caste" is a <u>silly</u> and <u>offensive</u> way of describing mixed-race people.
3) He <u>challenges</u> people to <u>reassess</u> how they see each other.

Not my Business (Pages 42-43)

1) The poet shows how <u>terrible</u> it is to be ruled by a violent regime.
2) He says that if people <u>ignore</u> what's happening to their neighbours, things will get worse and eventually <u>everyone</u> will suffer.
3) He encourages people to <u>stand up</u> for each other, in order to create a <u>better society</u>.

Two Scavengers in a Truck... (Pages 16-17)

1) There's a clear <u>division</u> between the two pairs of people in the poem.
2) The scavengers can only <u>stare</u> at the couple in the Merc and <u>imagine</u> what it would be like to live like them — they can never cross the "small gulf" between them.
3) The poet <u>criticises American society</u> for not doing anything about this <u>social divide</u>. His reference to "democracy" is sarcastic.

*Some people are **On Their Own***

Island Man (Pages 6-7)

1) This poem is about an <u>individual</u> who feels on his own.
2) The man in "Island Man" has a clear sense of <u>where he belongs</u>, i.e. in the Caribbean, not in London.
3) It's a fairly straightforward and familiar story of being <u>homesick</u>.

Hurricane Hits England (Pages 46-47)

1) Although <u>millions</u> of people were affected by the 1987 storm, the poet in "Hurricane Hits England" talks about her own <u>personal experience</u> of it.
2) The storm triggers a <u>moment of realisation</u> that changes the way she approaches life.
3) The storm makes her see that it <u>doesn't make sense</u> to feel homesick, because all parts of the Earth are <u>connected</u> to each other.

We are all individuals

'Presents from my Aunts' (pages 44-45), 'Night of the Scorpion' (18-19) and 'Vultures' (20-21) are also good poems for this topic. All the people in these poems encounter <u>problems</u> of some sort — you could compare someone who <u>solves their problems</u> with someone who <u>can't</u>, and discuss why.

Practice Questions — *People*

If the poem is about a person, you could discuss whether you identify with the person and their viewpoint or not. This shows the examiner that you're engaging with the poem.

These Poems are about People:

Island Man (pages 6-7)
Two Scavengers in a Truck... (pages 16-17)
Night of the Scorpion (pages 18-19)
Vultures (pages 20-21)
Search For My Tongue (pages 28-29)

Half-Caste (pages 32-33)
Not my Business (pages 42-43)
Presents from my Aunts... (pages 44-45)
Hurricane Hits England (pages 46-47)

1   Write a paragraph about a person who is important to you.

....

....

....

....

....

2   Pick a poem from the top of the page that you know well.
     What impression does the poet create of the person or people in this poem?

....

....

....

....

....

3   Choose a character or group of characters from a different poem.
     How does this character/group of characters interact with other people in society?

....

....

....

....

....

First Person

If a poet writes in the <u>first person</u>, they use words like "<u>I</u>" and "<u>me</u>", rather than "she" or "him".

> 1) Writing in the first person allows the poet to <u>use their voice directly</u>.
>
> 2) This allows them to say <u>how they feel</u> and <u>what they mean</u>.
>
> 3) The first person lets us see things from the poet or character's <u>point of view</u>.

Some poets "Look Inside Themselves"

Presents from my Aunts in Pakistan (Pages 44-45)

1) The first person perspective in this poem lets us see how <u>confused</u> and <u>uncertain</u> the girl is.
2) Phrases like "I could never be as lovely / as those clothes" (lines 18-19) give us an insight into her <u>emotions</u> that wouldn't be possible without the first person style.

Search For My Tongue (Pages 28-29)

1) The poet uses a <u>conversational</u> tone ("You ask me what I mean"), so that it sounds like she's explaining her thoughts to you, as if you're a <u>friend</u>.
2) Her descriptions of her <u>dreams</u> give us an idea of how her mind works.
3) This is important to the idea that her mother tongue is <u>living inside her</u>.

This Room (Pages 40-41)

1) The poem's about a very <u>personal</u> experience.
2) The poet uses the first person perspective to show us how <u>important</u> the event is to her.
3) <u>Surreal images</u> like her hands being "outside, clapping" show the weird <u>feelings</u> she's experiencing.

Some poets want to Inform or Persuade

Nothing's Changed (Pages 8-9)

1) The poet's voice allows us to experience the <u>inequality</u> through <u>his eyes</u>.
2) He sees the <u>luxury</u> of the whites-only inn — "I press my nose / to the clear panes" (lines 27-28) — but knows he's not welcome there.
3) He wants us to realise how <u>unfair</u> it is.
4) Using the first person makes his <u>message</u> more effective.

Not my Business (Pages 42-43)

1) The poet adopts the <u>persona</u> of a man who <u>doesn't get involved</u> when people are abused.
2) He shows the <u>selfishness</u> of this attitude — "What business of mine is it...?"
3) By showing that this mentality is <u>flawed</u>, the poet tries to <u>convince</u> people to do the <u>opposite</u> of what the man does, and stand up for each other.

Night of the Scorpion (Pages 18-19)

1) We see events unfold through the eyes of a <u>child</u> — "I watched the holy man perform his rites" (line 42).
2) He's <u>scared</u> and <u>confused</u> by the religious response to his mother being stung by the scorpion.
3) The poet uses the first person to show how <u>confusing</u> and illogical this response seems to him. He sees it as <u>superstitious</u> and <u>unhelpful</u>.

The first person lets the poet speak directly to the reader

'Limbo' (pages 4-5) 'Half-Caste' (32-33) and 'Hurricane...' (46-47) also use the first person.
It makes a massive difference to the <u>effect</u> of the poem, as it lets the poet talk <u>personally</u> — poems like "Not my Business" would really <u>lose their impact</u> if it was just "he" or "she" instead of "I".

Practice Questions — *First Person*

Poems written in the first person give the reader an insight into what the poet is feeling, and a chance to see events through the poet's eyes — make sure you can talk about the effects of writing in the first person.

These Poems use the First Person:

Limbo (pages 4-5)
Nothing's Changed (pages 8-9)
Night of the Scorpion (pages 18-19)
Search For My Tongue (pages 28-30)
Half-Caste (pages 32-33)

This Room (pages 40-41)
Not my Business (pages 42-43)
Presents from my Aunts in Pakistan (pages 44-45)
Hurricane Hits England (pages 46-47)

1   Describe two reasons why you think a poet might decide to write in the first person.

1) ....

....

....

2) ....

....

....

2   Choose a poem that you know from the top of the page.
     How does using the first person make the poem's message more effective?

....

....

....

....

....

....

3   Choose a different poem. Why do you think the poet has chosen to use the first person
     in this poem?

....

....

....

....

....

Specific Cultural References

Culture can be described as all the things which make up a community's <u>way of life</u>. Specific cultural references can be to beliefs, customs, religions, history, literature and loads of other things.

> 1) There can be <u>different cultures</u> within the <u>same society</u>.
>
> 2) Some people can grow up <u>surrounded</u> by a particular culture <u>without</u> really feeling <u>part of it</u>.
>
> 3) Some cultures <u>classify</u> people according to things like <u>race</u>, <u>gender</u> and <u>wealth</u>, rather than believing that everyone is equal.

Some cultures are Divided

Two Scavengers in a Truck... (Pages 16-17)

1) The <u>language</u> of the poem, e.g. "downtown" and "garbage truck", is strongly associated with <u>American culture</u>.
2) The culture of the USA claims to value <u>equal opportunity</u> and <u>democracy</u>.
3) But it seems the binmen will <u>never be able</u> to live like the rich couple.
4) So the <u>image</u> we have of American culture, where supposedly "everything is always possible" (line 30), is shown to be <u>false</u>.

Nothing's Changed (Pages 8-9)

1) The culture here is the divided society of modern <u>South Africa</u>. The poet mentions that it's District Six because this is the area he knows, but it applies to the <u>whole country</u>.
2) The idea of <u>racial segregation</u> is familiar when thinking of the country under apartheid, but the fact that it <u>still exists</u> under Mandela's rule seems <u>shocking</u>.
3) There's the odd use of South African <u>slang</u>, such as "boy" and "bunny chows", which adds to the feel of the poem being relevant <u>specifically</u> to South Africa.

Limbo (Pages 4-5)

1) The theme here is <u>slavery</u>. Although it was abolished in the 19th century, the <u>history</u> of slavery is still <u>important</u> to many black people today.
2) There are references to life as a slave, such as the <u>cramped conditions</u> on the slave ships.
3) The <u>limbo dance</u> is strongly linked to this West Indian slave culture.

People can become Separated from Their Culture

Night of the Scorpion (Pages 18-19)

1) It's set in a <u>Hindu</u> community in India.
2) The locals believe in <u>reincarnation</u>. The prayers relate to <u>purifying the soul</u> for the next life.
3) But the boy's father is a "sceptic", so the boy's probably grown up in a <u>non-religious</u> household — which must make the Hindu ceremony seem very <u>odd</u>.

Hurricane Hits England (Pages 46-47)

1) Before the storm, the poet has been feeling like an <u>outsider</u> to English culture.
2) She refers to African and Mayan <u>storm gods</u> — Huracan, Oya and Shango.
3) The poet uses the gods as a link to her <u>Caribbean roots</u> — the Caribbean was historically affected by Mayan culture, and many Africans were transported to the Caribbean during the slave trade.

Culture can be the central theme or provide the setting

'What Were They Like?' (pages 22-23), 'Search For My Tongue' (28-29), 'Not my Business' (42-43), and 'Presents from my Aunts in Pakistan' (pages 44-45) also fit into this topic. There are loads of <u>different cultures</u> in the anthology, which means there's plenty of <u>variety</u> to keep you <u>on your toes</u>.

Practice Questions — *Specific Cultural References*

Sometimes the poet uses language and dialect to refer to a specific culture. Look carefully at the poems and you should be able to work out which culture they're talking about.

These Poems have Specific Cultural References:

Limbo (pages 4-5)
Nothing's Changed (pages 8-9)
Two Scavengers in a Truck... (pages 16-17)
Night of the Scorpion (pages 18-19)
What Were They Like? (pages 22-23)

Search For My Tongue (pages 28-29)
Not my Business (pages 42-43)
Presents from my Aunts in Pakistan (pages 44-45)
Hurricane Hits England (pages 46-47)

1   Describe a culture that you feel part of, or that you have experienced.

   ....

   ....

   ....

   ....

   ....

   ....

2   Pick one of the poems with specific cultural references. Which culture does the poet describe in that poem, and what impression do we get of this culture?

   ....

   ....

   ....

   ....

   ....

3   Choose another poem from the box.
   How important to the poem's message is the culture described?

   ....

   ....

   ....

   ....

   ....

Description

Poets use various ways of <u>describing</u> things to keep the reader <u>interested</u>.

> 1) Poets can use exciting or unexpected <u>adjectives</u> to describe things or people.
>
> 2) They can use <u>comparisons</u>, strong <u>opinions</u> or <u>humour</u> if they want to give a particular <u>impression</u> of something or someone.
>
> 3) Contrasting descriptions can be used to show <u>differences</u> between people or places.

Poets describe People

Two Scavengers in a Truck... (Pages 16-17)

1) There's a sharp <u>contrast</u> between the <u>appearances</u> of the "grungy" binmen and the "elegant couple".
2) There's also a <u>suggested</u> contrast between <u>how hard</u> the two pairs of people <u>work</u> — the "scavengers" have been "up since 4 a.m.", while the driver of the Mercedes is still "on the way" to work.
3) <u>Contradictory</u> descriptions of the rich couple sometimes suggest <u>falseness</u> or <u>dishonesty</u>, e.g. "casually coifed" — "coifed" suggests time and effort, so the woman's casual image is <u>fake</u>.

Presents from my Aunts in Pakistan (Pages 44-45)

1) The poet's descriptions of the <u>presents</u> show her mixed feelings.
2) They're "<u>lovely</u>" but also "<u>broad and stiff</u>", showing they're <u>uncomfortable</u>.
3) Similes such as "glistening like an orange" show they also seem <u>exotic</u> to her, rather than normal.
4) Descriptions of <u>one thing</u> often also apply to <u>another</u>, e.g. Pakistan is "fractured", like her identity.

Blessing (Pages 10-11)

1) The descriptions of the <u>rush for water</u> from the burst pipe show how <u>desperate</u> the people are.
2) They have "frantic hands", which shows the <u>urgency</u> with which they collect the water.
3) The water is described as "fortune" and "silver", showing how <u>valuable</u> it is.
4) <u>Basic items</u> like "a tin mug" and "plastic buckets" seem to be the only possessions they own and they live in "huts", which emphasises how <u>poor</u> the slum-dwellers are.

Poets describe Places

Nothing's Changed (Pages 8-9)

1) The poet's descriptions of "hard stones", "seeding grasses" and "amiable weeds" in the first verse give an impression of District Six being <u>neglected</u> and <u>run-down</u>.
2) The <u>differences</u> between the lives of whites and blacks are shown by the contrast between the "<u>haute cuisine</u>" at the "up-market" inn and the "<u>bunny chows</u>" eaten at "a plastic table's top" at the cafe.

Island Man (Pages 6-7)

1) The "emerald island" of the Caribbean, with its "wild seabirds", sounds like an <u>unspoilt paradise</u>.
2) In contrast, the "grey metallic soar" of London traffic sounds <u>dreary and unnatural</u>.
3) We only hear the <u>good things about the Caribbean</u> and the <u>bad things about London</u>, which makes us realise he's longing to be back home.

Compare the different descriptions in a poem

Poets use descriptions to make their poems more interesting to read. Poets can use a lot of descriptions which <u>complement</u> each other to create an <u>overall impression</u> of something. But also look out for descriptions which <u>contrast</u> with something else in another part of the poem.

Practice Questions — *Description*

Without description poetry wouldn't be poetry — look at the adjectives the poets use, as they often give words lots of different meanings.

These Poems use Detailed Description:

Island Man (pages 6-7)
Nothing's Changed (pages 8-9)
Blessing (pages 10-11)
Two Scavengers in a Truck... (pages 16-17)

Night of the Scorpion (pages 18-19)
Vultures (pages 20-21)
Presents from my Aunts... (pages 44-45)

1   Think about the funniest thing you've ever seen. Describe it in a brilliant and poetic way.

....

....

....

....

....

....

2   Choose a poem which uses detailed description.
How effective do you think the poet's use of description is?

....

....

....

....

....

3   Choose another poem. How do we get a sense of the poet's opinion through her / his descriptions?

....

....

....

....

....

Metaphor

A <u>metaphor</u> is when something is described as if it's <u>something else</u> for effect.

> 1) Metaphors can be used to <u>emphasise</u> just how big, fast, fat, brilliant, rubbish or weird something or someone is.
>
> 2) <u>Extended</u> metaphors (also called <u>running</u> metaphors) are when a writer takes a metaphor and keeps going with it, applying <u>different aspects</u> of the metaphor to the thing being described.

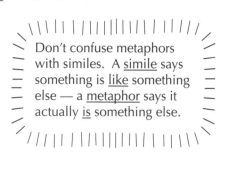

Don't confuse metaphors with similes. A <u>simile</u> says something is <u>like</u> something else — a <u>metaphor</u> says it actually <u>is</u> something else.

Metaphors can describe **People's Lives**

Vultures (Pages 20-21)

1) The vultures are ugly, <u>disgusting</u> creatures, but they're still capable of <u>gentleness</u>.
2) This leads to the description of the Commandant, who <u>murders</u> people every day yet <u>loves his child</u>.
3) So the <u>vultures</u> are a metaphor for the Commandant — although we <u>don't realise</u> this at first, as more than half the poem has passed before the Commandant is mentioned.

Blessing (Pages 10-11)

1) Water is described as "fortune" and "silver", showing how <u>valuable</u> it is to the people of the slum.
2) The people become a "congregation", creating a <u>religious</u> feel — they're <u>worshipping</u> this gift from "a kindly god".
3) The metaphor "the blessing sings / over their small bones" (lines 22 and 23) to describe the burst water pipe reinforces the <u>miraculous</u> feel of the poem's title and also how <u>vulnerable</u> the children are.

Metaphors can describe **Feelings**

This Room (Pages 40-41)

1) The <u>room</u> and the <u>furniture</u> become <u>alive</u>. This shows how the poet feels suddenly <u>free</u> after the special event that's happened.
2) The fact that such <u>ordinary</u> objects are "rising up to crash through clouds" (line 9) shows how <u>extraordinary</u> the situation is.
3) At the end of the poem, individual <u>parts of the poet's body</u> become independent, living things — maybe showing how <u>dizzy</u> and <u>disoriented</u> she is by all the excitement and how free she now feels.

Search For My Tongue (Pages 28-29)

1) The poet's <u>mother tongue</u> (Gujarati) is described as a <u>living thing</u> — she's worried that it will "rot and die".
2) This idea becomes a <u>running metaphor</u>. Gujarati is described metaphorically as a <u>flower</u>, and words like "bud" and "blossoms" show that it's <u>growing back</u>.
3) This creates the impression that her mother tongue is <u>rooted</u> in her.

Half-Caste (Pages 32-33)

1) The poet <u>mocks</u> the term "half-caste" by comparing mixed-race people to classical music and paintings — the idea of calling these things "half" just because they're mixed seems <u>absurd</u>.
2) He then uses the "half" idea to describe <u>body parts</u>, e.g. "I offer yu half-a-hand". This could be seen as a <u>metaphor</u> for the poet being <u>less than welcoming</u> to people with certain points of view.
3) He mixes in <u>humour</u> with his metaphors, so that his point about the <u>stupidity</u> of the word is clear.

Metaphors make poems more interesting

Remember to say <u>why</u> you think a poet has chosen to use a particular metaphor. Think about what <u>impression</u> the metaphor gives. If you can work this out, it's a big clue to the poet's <u>message</u>.

Practice Questions — *Metaphor*

You won't get many marks if you just identify the metaphors a poet uses — you need to say what effect they have on the reader. Use these questions to help form your ideas.

These Poems make strong use of Metaphor:

Limbo (pages 4-5)
Nothing's Changed (pages 8-9)
Blessing (pages 10-11)
Vultures (pages 20-21)

Search For My Tongue (pages 28-29)
Half-Caste (pages 32-33)
Love After Love (pages 34-35)
This Room (pages 40-41)

1   Why do you think poets sometimes choose to use a metaphor instead of describing something literally?

....

....

....

....

....

....

2   Select a poem from the box above and explain why the poet's use of metaphors is effective.

....

....

....

....

....

....

3   Explain how the poet uses metaphors to create a particular impression in one of the other poems.

....

....

....

....

....

Unusual Presentation

A lot of these poems have an <u>odd layout</u>. This might look daft at first, but it can be very effective.

> 1) The way a poem looks on the page affects your <u>first impressions</u> of it.
>
> 2) <u>Regular</u> styles of presentation tend to create a certain effect <u>throughout</u> the poem.
>
> 3) <u>Irregular</u> layout can create different effects in different parts of the poem.

Presentation can create an *Overall Effect*

What Were They Like? *(Pages 22-23)*

1) The questions and answers are <u>numbered</u> so that it looks like a 'real' enquiry.
2) Each question can be <u>matched</u> to its corresponding answer.
3) Each pair covers a <u>particular aspect</u> of the Vietnamese culture.
4) When you read a question and then its answer, <u>meanings</u> of certain words <u>change subtly</u>, e.g. "bone" in Q4 and A4 — this adds to the <u>uncertain tone</u>.
5) The <u>failure</u> to come up with any satisfactory answers adds to the sense of the poet's <u>condemnation</u> of the war.

Unrelated Incidents *(Pages 30-31)*

1) The <u>short lines</u> of almost even length make the poem look like a newsreader's <u>autocue</u>.
2) This adds <u>humour</u> to the poem, by creating a <u>visual impression</u> of the theme it discusses.
3) It's being read as if it's the news, so it sounds like the <u>truth</u> — the newsreader presents his views as <u>fact</u> rather than opinion.

Presentation can allow for *Different Effects*

Limbo *(Pages 4-5)*

1) There's a lot of <u>variance</u> between <u>line lengths</u> — some lines are quite long, others are only one word.
2) The <u>longer</u> lines, e.g. line 7, create an impression of the <u>ongoing cruelty</u> of slave conditions.
3) Shorter lines describe movement, e.g. the <u>repetition</u> of "down" makes it feel like an <u>ongoing</u> descent.
4) The repeated "limbo like me" lines are in <u>italics</u> to emphasise the <u>rhythm</u> of the <u>dance</u> that is always in the background.

Search For My Tongue *(Pages 28-29)*

1) Seeing the <u>Gujarati script</u> allows us to see how <u>different</u> it is from English.
2) This gives us an insight into <u>why</u> it's so <u>important</u> to the poet — it represents a <u>different side</u> of her personality.
3) The Gujarati words are spelt out <u>phonetically</u> too, so we can hear what they <u>sound like</u>.

Presentation can reflect the poem's theme

'Two Scavengers in a Truck, Two Beautiful People in a Mercedes' (pages 16-17), and 'Presents from my Aunts in Pakistan' (44-45) also have unusual presentation. It's all about creating a <u>visual effect</u>, to add to the effect of the words and sounds, and <u>illustrate</u> whatever point the poet is making.

Practice Questions — *Unusual Presentation*

These questions are to help you form your own ideas about the presentation a poet uses — try to answer them without referring too much to the page opposite.

These Poems have Unusual Presentation:

Limbo (pages 4-5)
Two Scavengers in a Truck... (pages 16-17)
What Were They Like? (pages 22-23)
Search For My Tongue (pages 28-29)

Unrelated Incidents (pages 30-31)
Presents from my Aunts... (pages 44-45)

1   Why do you think a poet might decide to use an unusual style of presentation?

....

....

....

....

....

....

2   Explain what effect the style of presentation has in one of the poems that you are familiar with from the box above.

....

....

....

....

....

....

3   Now pick another poem. How does the unusual presentation reflect the poem's theme?

....

....

....

....

Non-Standard English

Standard English means talking in a 'posh' accent, using "correct" grammar and no slang.
So non-standard English means anything else.

1) Non-standard English can mean talking in a regional accent, like Scouse or Geordie.

2) It includes using different forms of grammar, like West Indian Creole.

3) Slang words and swearing are non-standard English.

4) Non-standard English can mean being creative with the words you use.

Language links a poem with its Background

Limbo (Pages 4-5)

1) The poet uses the West Indian Creole dialect that slaves spoke in.
2) This links the poem with slave history, and allows the poet to write from a slave's point of view.
3) The simplified grammar of Creole gives the poem a harsh sound, e.g. "stick hit sound" —
   this reflects the harsh cruelty of slave punishment.

Island Man (Pages 6-7)

1) Words are used in unconventional ways, creating a confused feel in the language.
2) "Wombing" is used to describe the gentle, comforting sounds of the sea, but it also
   connects the sea to the man's birth, showing it's where he belongs.
3) The word "sands" is used to show that he's still thinking of the Caribbean,
   even though he's living in London.
4) Some words could apply to aspects of life in both the Caribbean and London,
   e.g. "roar" is used to describe the London traffic, but it also sounds like the sea.

Dialect can be In-Yer-Face

Unrelated Incidents (Pages 30-31)

1) The whole poem is written phonetically to represent a Glaswegian accent.
2) This emphasises how different it sounds to standard English.
3) Dialect is the subject of the poem. The newsreader believes that regional
   accents are inferior, but he is talking in one, which is pretty ironic.
4) The poet shows he's not ashamed to speak in his natural voice — he wants it
   to be heard, because he thinks we hear enough posh accents in public life.

Half-Caste (Pages 32-33)

1) The West Indian dialect sounds more direct than standard English,
   so the poet can challenge the reader, e.g. "wha yu mean".
2) Non-standard English allows the reader to 'hear' the poet's voice,
   so it feels more like a conversation.
3) The mixture of standard and non-standard English reflects the
   poet's mixed background, and shows that he's proud of it.

De language adds to de effeck

With poems like 'Half-Caste', it's easy to think the poet's just showing off by writing in dialect.
But the poems really wouldn't be very effective if they just said, "In my opinion, it's perfectly
acceptable to speak in dialect," or something like that. The sound of the poem when it's spoken is vital.

Practice Questions — *Non-Standard English*

Reading non-standard English can be tricky at first — but it often tells you quite a lot about the poet. It's worth reading through the poems that use non-standard English again to make sure you understand them.

> ## These Poems use Non-Standard English:
> Limbo (pages 4-5)   Unrelated Incidents (pages 30-31)
> Island Man (pages 6-7)   Half-Caste (pages 32-33)

1   What do you think non-standard English is?

....

....

....

....

....

....

2   Choose a poem that you know from the top of the page.
     Why do you think the poet has chosen to write in non-standard English in this poem?

....

....

....

....

....

....

3   Now look at one of the other poems.
     How important is the style of language to the impact of the poem?

....

....

....

....

....

....

Particular Places

The descriptions of <u>places</u> are strongly linked to the <u>message</u> of some of these poems.

> 1)   Some poets describe their <u>homes</u> or <u>birthplaces</u>.
> 2)   Other poets use a setting as a background for the <u>topic</u> they want to talk about.
> 3)   Places aren't always described in detail — sometimes a <u>lack of detail</u> can be effective.

Places can be connected to *Identity*

Presents from my Aunts in Pakistan (Pages 44-45)

1)   The poet only <u>vaguely</u> remembers Pakistan — she relies on <u>photos</u> and <u>newspapers</u> to describe it.
2)   Pakistan is described as "fractured", reflecting the poet's <u>split identity</u>.
3)   The poet's <u>personal</u> memories of Pakistan are of <u>mysterious</u> "shaded rooms" and beggars.
4)   These aren't very positive thoughts — she's <u>uncomfortable</u> with the idea of being Pakistani.

Hurricane Hits England (Pages 46-47)

1)   The woman wants to feel "closer / To the landscape" — she feels <u>emotional</u> about places.
2)   At the start of the poem, she feels a <u>long way</u> from her home in the Caribbean.
3)   When England gets a taste of a Caribbean-style storm, it makes her realise that <u>everywhere on Earth is connected</u> — so places aren't that important after all.

Places can stand for the *State of Society*

Two Scavengers in a Truck... (Pages 16-17)

1)   It's San Francisco, though it could be <u>many places in America</u>.
2)   The description of the setting in lines 1-2 sounds <u>unremarkable</u>, suggesting the situation the poet describes is not unusual — this is normal, <u>everyday life</u>.
3)   The situation represents the poet's views on <u>America</u> in general, and the <u>inequalities</u> he sees in its capitalist "democracy".

Nothing's Changed (Pages 8-9)

1)   Harsh-sounding descriptions of stones and weeds <u>set the tone</u> for the <u>bitterness</u> of the poem.
2)   The poet instinctively <u>recognises</u> his home district — "my feet know, / and my hands".
3)   The <u>neglected</u> condition of District Six and the <u>segregation</u> that still exists there represent the situation in the <u>whole of South Africa</u>.
4)   There's a clear <u>division</u> in one street — the plush inn at one end, and the grimy cafe, "down the road". This shows how the blacks and whites live <u>very close</u> to each other, but live <u>separate</u> lives.

Vultures (Pages 20-21)

1)   Bleak descriptions of the <u>vultures' habitat</u> create a <u>dark, miserable mood</u>.
2)   The poem starts at dawn, but there's only "greyness" and "drizzle" — there's <u>no sign of the sun</u>.
3)   There's <u>no other life</u> in this place — just a "dead tree", introducing the theme of <u>death</u>.
4)   The <u>dark, evil atmosphere</u> of the setting provides the perfect background for the <u>human evil</u> that the poem goes on to discuss.

Find out some bits and pieces about the setting

Often the setting is just a <u>backdrop</u> to the poem's issues. But in some poems, for example 'Hurricane Hits England', it's the <u>main theme</u>, so it's useful to know a few more details about these places.

Practice Questions — *Particular Places*

Look carefully at the setting the poet uses as it's sometimes easy to miss — make sure you have some ideas for a couple of the poems below.

> ### These Poems are about Particular Places:
>
> Nothing's Changed (pages 8-9)
> Island Man (pages 6-7)
> Blessing (pages 10-11)
> Two Scavengers in a Truck... (pages 16-17)
>
> Vultures (pages 20-21)
> What Were They Like? (22-23)
> Presents from my Aunts... (pages 44-45)
> Hurricane Hits England (pages 46-48)

1   Write a couple of sentences to describe your favourite place.

....

....

....

....

....

....

2   Choose a poem from the blue box at the top of the page.
    What kind of image do you get of the place described in the poem?

....

....

....

....

....

3   Choose another poem. Why is the setting important to the impact of the poem?

....

....

....

....

....

....

Two Cultures

Some of the poets talk about the effects of having <u>two different cultures</u> in their lives.

> 1) Having a <u>mixed background</u> can make people feel like they're <u>torn</u> between two cultures.
> 2) Sometimes people have <u>moved</u> to a different country and <u>miss</u> the culture they're <u>used to</u>.
> 3) Some cultures are <u>divided</u>, with one subculture <u>dominating</u> another.

Some cultures *Clash*

Search For My Tongue (Pages 28-29)

1) The poet sees the English and Asian cultures as being <u>separate parts of her</u>, that <u>can't</u> be brought together.
2) This <u>opposition</u> is shown through <u>languages</u> — her mother tongue (Gujarati) "could not really know the other" (English).
3) By the end of the poem, the two languages seem to be <u>fighting each other</u> — Gujarati "ties the other tongue in knots".

Unrelated Incidents (Pages 30-31)

1) The two cultures in this poem are <u>posh English</u> culture and <u>working-class Scottish</u> culture.
2) Again, the division is shown through <u>language</u> — standard BBC English versus regional accents. The poet believes that people <u>dismiss</u> regional accents as <u>inferior</u>.
3) The poet <u>stands up</u> for his own background, by criticising the <u>dominance</u> of posh English voices.

Presents from my Aunts in Pakistan (Pages 44-45)

1) The poet has spent most of her life in <u>England</u>, so the presents from <u>Pakistan</u> seem <u>foreign</u> to her, even though she was born in Pakistan and has relatives there.
2) The poet feels that the two cultures <u>don't mix well</u> — she feels "alien in the sitting-room" when she tries on the Pakistani clothes.
3) The realisation that she belongs to two cultures seems to <u>confuse</u> her rather than help her — at the end she seems to feel like an <u>outsider to both</u>.

Cultures can *Mix Together*

Half-Caste (Pages 32-33)

1) The poet in "Half-Caste" believes cultures <u>can mix together</u>.
2) The theme is that it's <u>good</u> when <u>cultures mix</u> — he compares it to "when light an shadow / mix in de sky", suggesting it's <u>natural</u>.
3) The poet seems <u>proud</u> of his own <u>mixed background</u>.

Hurricane Hits England (Pages 46-47)

1) The woman in the poem <u>doesn't feel a part</u> of English culture — she misses the Caribbean.
2) At the start of the poem, the cultures seem very <u>different</u>, and she feels a <u>long way from home</u>.
3) By the end, thanks to the storm gods, the poet sees all places and cultures as <u>being connected</u>, and suggests the differences <u>aren't important</u> after all — "the earth is the earth is the earth".

Belonging to two cultures can be good or bad

Some of the poets <u>like</u> having two cultures in their lives and some <u>don't</u>. Remember that everyone's background is <u>different</u>, so it's <u>not</u> as simple as some of them moaning about it and some of them making the most of it. Make sure you <u>know</u> how each poet feels about having two cultures in their lives.

Practice Questions — *Two Cultures*

Poets often use two cultures to show conflict, or two cultures coming together to create one person. Look at the poems below and decide whether they are showing conflict or resolution — use the questions below to help you.

These Poems are about Two Cultures:

Island Man (pages 6-7)
Search For My Tongue (pages 28-29)
Unrelated Incidents (pages 30-31)

Half-Caste (pages 32-33)
Presents from my Aunts in Pakistan (pages 44-45)
Hurricane Hits England (pages 46-47)

1   Do you feel that you belong to just one culture, or to more than one?

....

....

....

....

....

2   Pick a poem you've studied from the list above. Does the poet think that the two cultures can mix well or not? Explain your answer.

....

....

....

....

....

....

3   Select a second poem. How does this poet feel about cultures mixing together?

....

....

....

....

....

....

....

Universal Ideas

If something's <u>universal</u>, it could apply to <u>any place or time</u>, rather than being restricted to the exact situation in the poem. Many of these poets deal with universal themes.

> 1) Ideas like <u>loneliness</u>, <u>equality</u> and <u>identity</u> have interested people all over the world for ages.
>
> 2) Some poets talk about a <u>specific situation</u> as a way of making a point about people or society <u>in general</u>.

Some poets talk about **Equality**

Half-Caste *(Pages 32-33)*

1) This poem deals with ideas of <u>inferiority</u> and <u>equality</u>.
2) The poet thinks the expression "half-caste" suggests mixed-race people are <u>inferior</u>.
3) He <u>challenges</u> this viewpoint, sarcastically saying that he casts "half-a-shadow".
4) He <u>turns the idea around</u> by saying that it's the people who use the term "half-caste" who are <u>incomplete</u> because they don't use "de whole of yu mind".

Two Scavengers... *(Pages 16-17)*

1) The theme of this poem is how people allow <u>inequality</u> to happen.
2) This is a dig specifically at <u>American capitalist society</u>, but we know that inequality occurs to some extent in <u>any society</u>.
3) We see how the garbagemen are <u>fascinated</u> with the rich people, but the rich couple <u>aren't interested</u> in the garbagemen.
4) This suggests that people are <u>selfish</u>, and <u>ignore inequalities</u> — as long as they benefit from them.

Poems can be about aspects of **Humanity**

Love After Love *(Pages 34-35)*

1) This poem is about <u>being alone</u>.
2) The poet <u>challenges</u> the assumption that people are incomplete without <u>another person</u>.
3) The poet basically says you're often <u>better off on your own</u>. He advises the reader to "Give back your heart / To itself," as relationships can make you <u>betray your true identity</u>.

This Room *(Pages 40-41)*

1) The poem is about a <u>special moment</u> in life, when things suddenly <u>change for the better</u>.
2) We don't find out exactly what this moment is, and that adds to the universal feel of it — it stands for <u>any special, improbable event</u> in someone's life.
3) There's a sense of <u>optimism</u> about the poem — "This is the time and place / to be alive". The message is that you should <u>make the most</u> of opportunities when they come along.

Vultures *(Pages 20-21)*

1) It's about <u>good and evil</u>. The poet uses specific examples to move onto the topic in general.
2) Lines 22-29 are <u>universal</u>, and discuss how love and evil can exist separately in the same person.
3) Lines 41-51 are also universal, and sum up the theme of the poem. The poet asks whether we should be <u>grateful</u> that evil people are <u>capable of love</u>, or <u>depressed</u> because that love will always be <u>infected with evil</u>.

Specific examples can stand for things in general

Universal ideas are also dealt with in 'Nothing's Changed' (pages 8-9), 'Not my Business' (42-43) and 'Hurricane Hits England' (46-47). Make sure you can explain what all the universal themes are.

Practice Questions — *Universal Ideas*

Sometimes poets use specific situations to talk about the world in general. Make sure you study the poems carefully to find out what the poet is saying about the world.

These Poems are about Universal Ideas:

Nothing's Changed (pages 8-9)
Two Scavengers in a Truck... (pages 16-17)
Vultures (pages 20-21)
Half-Caste (pages 32-33)

Love After Love (pages 34-35)
This Room (pages 40-41)
Not my Business (pages 42-43)
Hurricane Hits England (pages 46-47)

1   Describe a film, TV programme, play or book that you have seen or read that made you think about a particular issue.

....

....

....

....

....

....

2   Choose a poem from the box at the top. What is the universal theme in the poem? How does the poet present this idea?

....

....

....

....

....

....

3   Choose another poem from the box.
How is the situation described in this poem relevant to more general issues?

....

....

....

....

....

Traditions

A <u>tradition</u> is a belief or custom that's been <u>passed down</u> from one generation to the next.

> 1) Some poets use traditions as a <u>link</u> to their <u>culture</u>, <u>past</u> or <u>identity</u>.
>
> 2) Sometimes they <u>criticise</u> traditions, seeing them as just silly <u>superstitions</u>.
>
> 3) Traditions can seem <u>distant</u> and <u>mysterious</u>.

Some traditions are *Mysterious*

Night of the Scorpion *(Pages 18-19)*

1) The poet describes traditional <u>Hindu</u> beliefs about <u>reincarnation</u>.
2) The villagers believe that the <u>pain</u> the boy's mother is feeling will mean her <u>next life</u> will be <u>better</u>.
3) The poet seems <u>separated</u> from this, probably because his dad isn't a Hindu believer.
   So these traditions appear <u>strange</u> and <u>superstitious</u> to him.
4) The poet's description of them calmly sitting in a <u>circle</u> around his mother, while she "twisted through and through", sounds <u>critical</u> — he wishes they would do something more <u>practical</u> to help her.

What Were They Like? *(Pages 22-23)*

1) The poem is about <u>Vietnamese</u> traditions and culture, written as though these are lost for ever.
2) The descriptions of these traditions have an <u>uncertain</u> feel to them, to emphasise that the war has destroyed this culture and its traditions for ever.
3) There's a <u>mysterious but beautiful</u> feel to this way of life — "stone lanterns illumined pleasant ways". This adds to the poet's <u>anger</u> at what has happened to Vietnam.
4) But there are also questions about <u>ceremonies</u> and <u>ornaments</u>, showing that they had plenty <u>in common with us</u> too.
5) "It is not remembered" whether they had an "epic poem". <u>Traditional stories</u> usually last for a very long time, but even these have disappeared, showing that all <u>links to the past</u> have been <u>lost</u>.

Traditions can provide a *Link with the Past*

Limbo *(Pages 4-5)*

1) Some people believe that the <u>limbo dance</u> originated from memories of being transported in cramped <u>slave ships</u>. Others believe it originated in <u>Africa</u> and was brought over by <u>slaves</u>.
2) It's now a traditional <u>West Indian</u> dance that celebrates black people's <u>survival</u> and <u>freedom</u>.
3) The poet uses the "*limbo like me*" refrain to emphasise his <u>links with black history</u>.
4) Slave history and traditions are linked to his <u>freedom</u> at the end of the poem, when "the drummers are praising me" — his <u>solidarity</u> with the slaves helps him <u>break free</u>.

Hurricane Hits England *(Pages 46-47)*

1) Traditional <u>Mayan</u> and <u>African</u> beliefs say that the weather is caused by <u>gods</u>.
2) The poet calls on the <u>storm gods</u> (Huracan, Oya and Shango) to explain <u>why</u> the hurricane has come to England.
3) The poet uses these gods as a <u>link</u> with her <u>Caribbean roots</u>. She feels a new sense of <u>freedom</u> and <u>purpose</u>.

Traditions can be described positively or negatively

Traditions are also explored in Presents from my Aunts in Pakistan (pages 44-45). Most of the poets have pretty strong opinions about tradition and culture — they're generally either <u>well into it</u>, or they think it's <u>a bit silly</u>, even if they don't say so outright.

Practice Questions — *Traditions*

This is the last set of questions on themes. Use the questions below to help form your own ideas about the traditions described in the poems in the box below.

These Poems are about Traditions:
Limbo (pages 4-5)   Presents from my Aunts in Pakistan (pages 44-45)
Night of the Scorpion (pages 18-19)   Hurricane Hits England (pages 46-47)
What Were They Like? (pages 22-23)

1   Describe a tradition that you take part in.

     ....

     ....

     ....

     ....

     ....

     ....

2   Pick a poem from the box and explain what impression the poet gives of the traditions
      they describe.

     ....

     ....

     ....

     ....

     ....

     ....

3   Choose another poem. What is the effect of the way traditions have been described?

     ....

     ....

     ....

     ....

     ....

Sample Essay and Exam Method: Identity

FOLLOW THIS FIVE-STEP METHOD FOR A DECENT ANSWER EVERY TIME

First, the basics. You get <u>45 minutes</u> for this question in the exam. It's <u>crucial</u> that you spend about <u>10 minutes</u> of this <u>planning</u> your answer — if you don't, your essay is likely to have a poor structure.

Remember — <u>every question</u> deals with a theme. The theme for this sample question is <u>identity</u>. Other <u>key words</u> in this question are "<u>ideas</u>" and "<u>feelings</u>". Refer to them throughout your essay. I've highlighted them in the sample answer on page 81.

1) Write a bit about the **Theme**

1)   Give a <u>definition</u> of the theme. You don't have to go into any detail — this example is quite basic.

2)   <u>Explain</u> how the theme relates to the poems you will write about.

2) Compare the **Structures** of each poem

1)   Say in <u>one sentence</u> how the structure of the two poems <u>relates to the theme of the question</u>.

2)   Look at the notes on each poem (pages 28-29 for 'Search...', and 44-45 for 'Presents...'). Use these to <u>explain</u> in more <u>detail</u> how the <u>structure</u> of the poems <u>relates</u> to the <u>theme in the question</u>. Write a <u>couple of sentences</u> about each poem.

3)   Write about any <u>similarities</u> and <u>differences</u> in the structure of the two poems.

You could write about some of these things, if any of them really stand out:

• Line length	• Rhyme or rhythm	• Symmetry	• Punctuation
• Stanza shape	• Repetition	• Narrative or timescale	• Layout

3) Compare the **Use of Language** in each poem

1)   Think about the "<u>Language</u>" parts of the pages on each poem (pages 28-29 for 'Search...', and 44-45 for 'Presents...').

2)   For each poem, pick the <u>type of fancy language</u> that <u>best relates to the theme</u>. Then, for <u>each</u> poem, write a couple of sentences about <u>how</u> this type of fancy language relates to the theme of the question.

3)   Explain any <u>similarities</u> and <u>differences</u> in the ways that the two poets use language in their poems.

• Images, similes and metaphors	• Powerful words	• Assonance	• Non-standard English
• Who is speaking	• Onomatopoeia	• Personification	• Contrasting ideas between poems
• Tone or atmosphere	• Alliteration	• Questions or commands	

4) Compare the **Feelings** of the poets

1)   Write <u>one sentence</u> about how the <u>feelings</u> of the poets are <u>similar or different</u>. Relate it to the <u>theme of the question</u>.

2)   Look at the "<u>Poet's Feelings and Attitudes</u>" parts of the poem pages. Pick the ones that <u>relate best</u> to the theme of the question. Write about the <u>similarities and differences</u> between the two poems.

5) Write about how the poem makes you **Feel**

1)   Say which poem you <u>preferred</u> and <u>why</u>.

2)   Say what you've <u>learnt</u> about the theme.

3)   Show some <u>empathy</u> — connect the poem to <u>your own feelings and experiences</u>.

Sample Essay and Exam Method: Identity

THIS SAMPLE ESSAY USES THE FIVE-STEP METHOD

Learn the stuff on your poems and themes, then use this method in the exam, and you'll be fine.

Question 1 Compare 'Presents from my Aunts in Pakistan' with one other poem, showing how the poets reveal ideas and feelings about their identity.

Our age, our gender, our social position and our personality make up our identity. Where we come from can also have a strong influence: the country or regions in which we grow up and live can have an important impact on how we see ourselves. In 'Search For My Tongue', it is language that is central to identity, whereas in 'Presents from my Aunts in Pakistan', dress and family customs are important ideas.

Talk about the theme straight away — that's what the question is about.

The poets structure their poems in different ways to express their ideas and feelings about identity. 'Search...' has a clear, three-part layout which shows the poet's feelings about her divided identity. The difficulties of being fluent in two languages are explained in lines 1-16. Lines 17-30, in Gujarati (with phonetic spelling), describe how the mother tongue returns during her dreams, and lines 31-38 are a 'translation' of the Gujarati. This structure reflects the problem of identity for the poet, as she has put the Gujarati tongue at the heart of the poem as it is at the heart of her being. In contrast, 'Presents...' has a very haphazard structure with varied line lengths and layout, reflecting the teenage girl's confusion over her identity.

Make sure you constantly refer to the key words in the question — I've highlighted them.

Metaphorical language is used in both poems to show the poets' ideas about identity. For instance, in 'Search...' there is an extended metaphor of the tongues being like plants growing in her mouth, with her mother tongue eventually dominating: it "grows longer, grows moist, grows strong veins, / it ties the other tongue in knots". This metaphor emphasises her feelings about her identity coming through her mother tongue. In "Presents..." the image of the snapped bangles suggests the girl wants to break free of her Pakistani identity. The fact that the bangles drew blood suggests how painful, physically and mentally, her torn identity is. The young girl in "Presents..." seems to want to escape from her cultural roots but, in contrast, Sujata Bhatt is delighted when her mother tongue returns.

Remember — you've got to compare and contrast the two poems all the time.

There are both similarities and differences in the ways that the poets use language to show their feelings about their identity. Both poets show regret at not having a clear sense of who they are or where they belong. The teenage girl in 'Presents...' tries on the Pakistani clothes but feels "alien in the sitting-room. I could never be as lovely / as those clothes". The word "alien" is particularly effective in expressing how unnatural and unhappy she feels. Similarly, Bhatt asks the reader to imagine the conflict between her two languages: "You could not use them both together". They also share the feelings of wanting to know their 'real' self. Bhatt is pleased when she realises, "Everytime I think I've forgotten, / I think I've lost the mother tongue, / it blossoms out of my mouth". However, in 'Presents...' the girl longs "for denim and corduroy" and realises she is "half-English, / unlike Aunt Jamila". The feelings each poet expresses about their identity have a link in that they both are uncertain about who they are, and regret the loss of their cultural roots. The difference is that in 'Search...' the woman's mother tongue returns to her and she feels happy: "it blossoms out of my mouth", but in 'Presents...' the girl doesn't feel completely comfortable with either her English or her Pakistani identity.

I enjoyed both these poems, but I preferred 'Presents...' as I feel it is easier to relate to the feelings in this poem. The way Sujata Bhatt discusses identity is quite specific, and difficult to relate to unless the reader also speaks two languages. I think that Moniza Alvi's description of the confusion of trying to work out who you really are, on the other hand, is a feeling that many of us can relate to, regardless of our background.

You've got to write about your feelings towards the poems. Don't worry if you don't feel anything — just write something believable.

Sample Essay and Exam Method: Description

THIS FIVE-STEP METHOD IS GOOD FOR A TOP-NOTCH ANSWER EVERY TIME

First, the basics. You get <u>45 minutes</u> for this question in the exam. It's <u>crucial</u> that you spend about <u>10 minutes</u> of this <u>planning</u> your answer — if you don't, your essay might be complete and utter rubbish.

Remember — <u>every question</u> deals with a theme. The theme for this sample question is <u>description</u>. Other <u>key words</u> in this question are "<u>thoughts</u>" and "<u>feelings</u>". Refer to them throughout your essay. I've highlighted them in the sample essay on the next page.

1) Write a bit about the **Theme**

1) Give a <u>definition</u>. You don't have to go into any detail — this example is quite straightforward.

2) <u>Explain</u> how the theme is used in the poems you will write about.

2) Compare the **Structures** of each poem

1) Say in <u>one sentence</u> how the structure of the two poems <u>relates to the theme of the question</u>.

2) Look at the notes on each poem (pages 8-9 for 'Nothing's Changed', and 10-11 for 'Blessing'). Use these to <u>explain</u> in more <u>detail</u> how the <u>structure</u> of the poems <u>relates</u> to the <u>theme in the question</u>. Write a <u>couple of sentences</u> about each poem.

3) Write about the <u>similarities</u> and <u>differences</u> in the structure of the two poems.

   You could write about some of these things, if any of them <u>really stand out</u>:

• Line length	• Rhyme or rhythm	• Symmetry	• Punctuation
• Stanza shape	• Repetition	• Narrative or timescale	• Layout

3) Compare the **Use of Language** in each poem

1) Look at the "<u>Language</u>" parts of the pages on each poem (pages 8-9 for 'Nothing's Changed', and 10-11 for 'Blessing').

2) For each poem, pick the <u>type of fancy language</u> that <u>best relates to the theme</u>. Then, for <u>each</u> poem, write a few sentences about <u>how</u> this type of fancy language relates to the theme of the question.

3) Explain the <u>similarities</u> and <u>differences</u> in the ways that the two poets use language in their poems.

• Images, similes and metaphors	• Powerful words	• Assonance	• Non-standard English
• Who is speaking	• Onomatopoeia	• Personification	• Contrasting ideas between poems
• Tone or atmosphere	• Alliteration	• Questions or commands	

4) Compare the **Feelings** of the poets

1) Write <u>one sentence</u> about how the <u>feelings</u> of the poets are <u>similar or different</u>. Relate it to the <u>theme of the question</u>.

2) Look at the "<u>Poet's Feelings and Attitudes</u>" parts of the poem pages. Pick the ones that <u>relate best</u> to the theme of the question. Write about the <u>similarities and differences</u> between the two poems.

5) Write about how the poem makes you **Feel**

1) Say which poem you <u>preferred</u> and <u>why</u>.

2) Say what you've <u>learnt</u> about the theme.

3) Show some <u>empathy</u> — connect the poem to <u>your own feelings and experiences</u>.

Sample Essay and Exam Method: Description

HERE'S ANOTHER EXAMPLE OF THE FIVE-STEP METHOD

Practise using this method to make sure you're ready for the exam.

Question 2	Compare 'Nothing's Changed' with one other poem, showing how the poets use description to convey their thoughts and feelings in their poems.

Description is a useful technique for poets to use as it enables the reader to visualise and understand the themes and ideas of a piece more clearly. In 'Nothing's Changed', description makes us realise the significance of District Six for this poet. In 'Blessing', descriptive techniques are used differently in order to recreate the people's feelings and actions, as well as creating a picture of their environment.

It's good to use the key words from the question because it shows that you are answering it directly.

The structure of 'Nothing's Changed' is based around the poet's return to District Six, and the descriptions are vital to our understanding of this event. As he walks through the area he recognises it instinctively but then is shocked by the "whites only inn". He becomes angry as he is effectively forced to go to the "working man's cafe", and this makes him remember all the past injustices. The structure of "Blessing" has a role in supporting the description. The four stanzas describe different aspects of the event. The descriptions in lines 12 to 23 are listed one after another, adding to the sense of the desperate action, as the villagers rush to collect the water with their "frantic hands". Reading the first and last lines of the poem together gives the disturbing simile, "The skin cracks like a pod/over their small bones".

Try and write a similar amount about each poem — this'll make sure that your answer is balanced.

There are many different descriptive devices used in both poems, and these emphasise the poets' thoughts and feelings about their subjects. 'Nothing's Changed' starts by using alliteration and onomatopoeia in short, harsh words such as "cuffs, cans" and "crunch". These words show the poet's feeling of brewing anger as well as the environment. The simile used to describe the hotel, "name flaring like a flag," reveals the arrogance of the white establishment. The images of glass describe a range of ideas: it is a barrier keeping him out — "I press my nose / to the clear panes"; it represents the white class drinking — "crushed ice white glass"; it reflects him as a "boy again"; and finally it is used to describe his intention to strike back, to "shiver down the glass" and all that it represents.

Using terms like onomatopoeia is good — it helps you to explain what you mean without waffling.

In "Blessing", methods of description are important to our understanding of the reactions of the local people to the burst pipe, their living conditions and how highly they value water. The simile, "The skin cracks like a pod", brings home the dryness. A sense of bustle is created when we hear, "a roar of tongues", as they shout and scream with delight at the sudden provision of water. Metaphors like "fortune" and "silver" are used to describe the value they put on water. The phrase "liquid sun" suggests its life-giving quality. These descriptions are most powerful when linked to their religion; there is "a congregation", who worship a "small splash" as "the voice of a kindly god". The poet clearly feels respect and admiration for this community and for their attitude to life in such difficult conditions.

There is a real difference in the descriptions of the thoughts and feelings expressed in these two poems. The poet in 'Nothing's Changed' is very much at the centre of the poem. The negative feelings of anger and bitter disappointment he describes here are very much his own, the "inwards turning / anger of my eyes." In contrast, 'Blessing' describes the celebratory thoughts and feelings of a group of people, "naked children / screaming in the liquid sun," as well as the understated concern and respect that the poet feels for them.

I found 'Nothing's Changed' more interesting than 'Blessing' because of the historical and political aspects. I have been impressed by how descriptive techniques used in poems like this can effectively recreate the different environments and also convey the thoughts and feelings of the poets. These poems have made me realise how fortunate I am to live in this country, where water is plentiful, and we can enjoy freedom and equality.

It looks good if you can relate the issues in the poem to your life — it shows that you appreciate what the poet is feeling.

Sample Essay and Exam Method: Politics

FOR A SUREFIRE QUALITY ANSWER, FOLLOW THE FIVE-STEP METHOD

First, the basics. You get <u>45 minutes</u> for this question in the exam. It's <u>crucial</u> that you spend about <u>10 minutes</u> of this <u>planning</u> your answer — if you don't, your essay will probably be drivel.

Remember — <u>every question</u> deals with a theme. The themes for this sample question are <u>politics</u> and <u>society</u>. Other <u>key words</u> in this question are "<u>attitudes</u>" and "<u>feelings</u>". Refer to them throughout your essay. I've highlighted them in the sample essay on the next page.

1) Write a bit about the **Theme**

1)   Give a <u>definition</u>. You don't have to go into lots of detail — this example is pretty simple.

2)   <u>Explain</u> how the theme is used in the poems you will write about.

2) Compare the **Structures** of each poem

1)   Say in <u>one sentence</u> how the structure of the two poems <u>relates to the theme of the question</u>.

2)   Look at the notes on each poem (pages 42-43 for 'Not my Business', and 30-31 for 'Unrelated Incidents'). Use these to <u>explain</u> in more <u>detail</u> about how the <u>structure</u> of the poems <u>relates</u> to the <u>theme in the question</u>. Write a <u>couple of sentences</u> about each poem.

3)   Write about the <u>similarities</u> and <u>differences</u> in the structure of the two poems.

You could write about some of these things, if any of them <u>really stand out</u>:

• Line length	• Rhyme or rhythm	• Symmetry	• Punctuation
• Stanza shape	• Repetition	• Narrative or timescale	• Layout

3) Compare the **Use of Language** in each poem

1)   Look at the "<u>Language</u>" parts of the pages on each poem (pages 42-43 for 'Not my Business', and 30-31 for 'Unrelated Incidents').

2)   For each poem, pick the <u>type of fancy language</u> that <u>best relates to the theme</u>. Then, for <u>each</u> poem, write a couple of sentences about <u>how</u> this type of fancy language relates to the theme of the question.

3)   Explain the <u>similarities</u> and <u>differences</u> in the ways that the two poets use language in their poems.

• Images, similes and metaphors	• Powerful words	• Assonance	• Non-standard English
• Who is speaking	• Onomatopoeia	• Personification	• Contrasting ideas between poems
• Tone or atmosphere	• Alliteration	• Questions or commands	

4) Compare the **Feelings** of the poets

1)   Write <u>one sentence</u> about how the <u>feelings</u> of the poets are <u>similar or different</u>. Relate it to the <u>theme of the question</u>.

2)   Look at the "<u>Poet's Feelings and Attitudes</u>" parts of the poem pages. Pick the ones that <u>relate best</u> to the theme of the question. Write about the <u>similarities and differences</u> between the two poems.

5) Write about how the poem makes you **Feel**

1)   Say which poem you <u>preferred</u> and <u>why</u>.

2)   Say what you've <u>learnt</u> about the theme.

3)   Show some <u>empathy</u> — connect the poem to <u>your own feelings and experiences</u>.

Sample Essay and Exam Method: Politics

THE FIVE STEP METHOD IS SIMPLE TO USE

Here's another example of how to use the five-step method.

Question 3   Compare 'Not my Business' with one other poem which demonstrates strong attitudes and feelings about how individuals are treated in society.

The political organisation of a country is not just about the type of government it has; it also involves how people in communities relate to each other. The UK is a democracy where rights are protected and everyone is considered equal, but some countries are dictatorships where people fear losing their freedom and even their lives.

> It's good to show that you understand the political circumstances that the poet is writing about.

In 'Not my Business', we hear the voice of an individual whose attitude is that it is best to stay out of politics. However, the poet's view is that everyone should be involved, otherwise people will end up being treated cruelly. 'Unrelated Incidents' is about people's attitudes towards language. It is about how British newsreaders usually talk in middle-class, English accents, and how in our society this accent is associated with power and authority. The poem highlights how people's voices and points of view can be marginalised if they speak in a working-class or regional accent.

Both poets use structure to convey their attitudes and feelings. The four stanzas of 'Not my Business' follow a narrative structure. Each stanza provides a different example of the brutality of the regime: "They picked Akanni up one morning / Beat him soft like clay". The first three stanzas have repeated lines at the end; in these lines, instead of facing up to the cruel treatment of his friends, he asks, "What business of mine is it...?" A pattern is established by the times of day referenced in each stanza, "They came one night...And then one evening". This shows that these people are never safe, whether it is day or night. In contrast, 'Unrelated Incidents' has a simple but unusual layout. It resembles a newsreader's autocue, so it relates to the subject. The short lines are startling but are used to make the poet's point about how regional dialects are not acceptable as carriers of the news, "yi / widny wahnt / mi ti talk / aboot thi / trooth wia / voice lik / wanna yoo / scruff". However, the short lines make it appear as if he is mocking 'normal language'.

> Make sure you include quotes to back up the points you are making.

The way that poetic devices are used in the poems differs. 'Not my Business' uses a range of techniques to emphasise the attitudes and feelings in the poem. The threat of violence is a constant theme. In the first stanza the simile describes how Akanni's body changes shape due to the beating. The metaphor that follows, "stuffed him down the belly / Of a waiting jeep," reinforces the idea of the regime being like a vicious predator. The use of personification in "bewildered lawn" suggests that even the country's landscape is affected by the regime's brutality. It shows how it is inescapable and maybe undefeatable. In contrast, the poetic devices used in 'Unrelated Incidents' are limited. The lack of punctuation and capital letters reinforces the poet's attempt to make fun of BBC English. The phonetic spelling is the most obvious device, which wittily allows us to try out his dialect and hear the ironic message he puts across: "thirza right / way ti spell / ana right way / ti tok it". He feels strongly that the educated, English middle classes hold power and exercise it through the way they speak. Their message to him and people like him is clear: "belt up".

> Make suggestions about why you think the poet has chosen to use particular poetic devices.

There are strong attitudes and feelings in both poems. Both poets express anger at the situations they describe. Osundare is not only angry at corrupt regimes, but also at the complacent attitudes of people who try and hide from such issues in society. The title is clearly ironic: it should be our business. Similarly, Tom Leonard is angry with the way people with local accents and dialects are seen as inferior to those who speak 'correctly'. We also sense the feelings of the characters in both poems. The man is obviously terrified that he will be taken next and experiences the guilt of inaction, whereas the "scruffs" in Leonard's poem feel inadequate and powerless because of society's attitude to how they speak.

I think it is important that people recognise and react to the inequalities in the way people are treated in society. 'Not my Business' demonstrates that people have a responsibility to protect and care about each other's rights. If we ignore abuses and inequalities they can become more widespread. British society can appear to be much fairer than the society described in 'Not my Business'. However, Tom Leonard's poem shows that inequalities do exist, such as the predominance of English, middle-class (BBC) accents as the voices of power and authority.

> Summarise the main points that you have made in your essay to draw everything to a conclusion.

Sample Essay and Exam Method: People

FOLLOW THIS FIVE-STEP METHOD FOR A DECENT ANSWER EVERY TIME

First, the basics. You get <u>45 minutes</u> for this question in the exam. It's <u>crucial</u> that you spend about <u>10 minutes</u> of this <u>planning</u> your answer — if you don't, your essay will be scuppered from the start. Remember — <u>every question</u> deals with a theme. The theme for this sample question is <u>people</u>. Other <u>key words</u> in this question are "<u>conflict</u>" and "<u>cultures</u>". Refer to them throughout your essay. I've highlighted them in the sample essay on the next page.

1) Write a bit about the **Theme**

1) Give a <u>definition</u>. It doesn't have to be technical — just describe what you think the theme means.

2) <u>Explain</u> how the theme is explored in the poems you will write about.

2) Compare the **Structures** of each poem

1) Say in <u>one sentence</u> how the structure of the two poems <u>relates to the theme of the question</u>.

2) Look at the notes on each poem (pages 6-7 for 'Island Man', and 16-17 for 'Two Scavengers...'). Use these to write about how the <u>structure</u> of the poems <u>relates</u> to the <u>theme in the question</u>. Write a <u>couple of sentences</u> about each poem.

3) Write about the <u>similarities</u> and <u>difference</u> in the structures of the two poems.

You could write about some of these things, if any of them <u>really stand out</u>:

• Line length	• Rhyme or rhythm	• Symmetry	• Punctuation
• Stanza shape	• Repetition	• Narrative or timescale	• Layout

3) Compare the **Use of Language** in each poem

1) Look at the "<u>Language</u>" parts of the pages on each poem (pages 6-7 for 'Island Man', and 16-17 for 'Two Scavengers...').

2) For each poem, pick the <u>type of fancy language</u> that <u>best relates to the theme</u>. Then, for <u>each</u> poem, write a couple of sentences about <u>how</u> this type of fancy language relates to the theme of the question.

3) Explain the <u>similarities</u> and <u>differences</u> in the ways that the two poets use language in their poems.

• Images, similes and metaphors	• Powerful words	• Assonance	• Non-standard English
• Who is speaking	• Onomatopoeia	• Personification	• Contrasting ideas between poems
• Tone or atmosphere	• Alliteration	• Questions or commands	

4) Compare the **Feelings** of the poets

1) Write <u>one sentence</u> about how the <u>feelings</u> of the poets are <u>similar or different</u>. Relate it to the <u>theme of the question</u>.

2) Look at the "<u>Poet's Feelings and Attitudes</u>" parts of the poem pages. Pick the ones that <u>relate best</u> to the theme of the question. Write about the <u>similarities and differences</u> between the two poems.

5) Write about how the poem makes you **Feel**

1) Say which poem you <u>preferred</u> and <u>why</u>.

2) Say what you've <u>learnt</u> about the theme.

3) Show some <u>empathy</u> — connect the poem to <u>your own feelings and experiences</u>.

Sample Essay and Exam Method: People

YOU CAN USE THE FIVE-STEP METHOD FOR ANY QUESTION

Here's one more example for you to have a look at.

Question 4 — Compare 'Island Man' with one other poem, to show how the poets use people to explain the conflict that can exist between and within different cultures.

People are at the centre of all communities. They embody the values, customs and ideas that a particular culture possesses. By examining how people behave and think, it is possible to gain a greater understanding of how their cultural roots affect them. 'Island Man' describes how an immigrant in London reacts to his environment as he dreams of his Caribbean home. In contrast, the people in 'Two Scavengers...' all live in San Francisco, but lead totally different lives there.

Try to establish why the theme is important in your opening paragraph.

'Island Man' uses structure to show the conflicting and confused waking thoughts of the man. There is no punctuation, the line lengths vary and some phrases are totally misplaced, as is the individual: "he always comes back   groggily groggily". Like 'Island Man', 'Two Scavengers...' also has no punctuation. It represents an instant in time, like the flash of a camera. The conflicting images seem to be laid one on top of the other, line by line, emphasising the contrasts between the two lifestyles.

Talk about the methods that the poets use to explore the themes.

The language in 'Island Man' shows the inner turmoil that the character is going through. The reader gets a series of contrasting images. For example, "the sound of blue surf" of the Caribbean conflicts with, the "grey metallic soar" of London. The "pillow waves" show the troubled sleep he has had which has caused the ruffles, but also tell of the dreams he has had of his "emerald island". The word "wombing" suggests the sense of security his homeland offers him, in contrast to the faceless "dull North Circular roar" of London. Contrast is also used in 'Two Scavengers...', but here it is the contrast of the different types of people: the woman is "casually coifed", the older man is "grungy". Although the young men's hair and glasses are similar, their appearances are mostly very different; the "hip three-piece linen suit" conflicts with the "red plastic blazers".

It will impress the examiner if you can show that you empathise with the characters in the poem.

The use of vocabulary is effective in both poems. Some words, such as "soar", "roar" and "surge" have double meanings: they are positive when they relate to his island, but have negative meanings in London. In 'Two Scavengers...', descriptive words are used to highlight the differences between the people. For example, "scavengers" are unworthy compared to "an elegant couple". The poet uses this contrast to make a direct criticism of society and how it creates this division between rich and poor people. Phrases like "small gulf" emphasise how these people may only be a few metres apart on the street, but, in terms of their lifestyles, they will never meet.

Both poets show how the people feel in their different situations and give us their own view. 'Island Man' obviously has fond memories of the Caribbean but resents his dull lifestyle in London. We can feel his depression as he "heaves himself" to "Another London day". Grace Nichols has sympathy for this man as he feels the conflict of these two cultures. The feelings revealed in 'Two Scavengers...' are very one-sided, as we have the envy of the poor, "as if they were watching some odorless TV ad / in which everything is always possible," contrasting with the uncaring attitude of the rich, who don't even seem to notice the truck or its passengers. The poet's attitude here is one of despair at this unequal society.

'Island Man' has made me more aware of how it might feel to be trapped in a foreign country, while 'Two Scavengers...' starkly highlights the divisions in American society. The poems have made me hope that in the future, society will be more equal and that governments who promise equal opportunities for all will deliver on what they say.

Try and work out what comment on society the author is making through their poem.

Identity and Politics

In this section, there are 28 practice exam questions for you to have a go at. Once you've spent some time on these, the questions you'll get in the real exam shouldn't scare you at all.

The practice exam questions are all helpfully arranged into themes. On this page are questions on identity and politics to get you started. Look at pages 52 and 54 for more on these themes and the poems to do with them. Good luck.

---

1   Compare how the poets present their ideas about identity in *Nothing's Changed* (page 8) and one other poem.

(27 marks)

---

2   In *Love After Love* (page 34), we see how a return to the true self is a cause of celebration.

Compare this to one other poem that is concerned with identity.

(27 marks)

---

3   Divisions in society are described in *Two Scavengers in a Truck...* (page 16).

Choose one other poem with a political theme and compare how the poets present their ideas.

(27 marks)

---

4   The mistreatment of individuals in society is described in *Not my Business* (page 42).

Compare this with one other poem which has a political theme.

(27 marks)

Change and People

On this page you'll find questions on <u>change</u> and <u>people</u>. Have a look at pages 56 and 58 if you can't remember what exactly these themes are. You'll also find lists of appropriate poems that you might want to talk about in your answers.

---

5 The poet in *Search For My Tongue* (page 28) is concerned about changes in her life.

Compare the view of change in this poem with the way change is presented in one other poem from the 'Different Cultures' section of the anthology.

(27 marks)

---

6 The poem *What Were They Like?* (page 22) addresses change in a community.

Compare it with one other poem which deals with the theme of change.

(27 marks)

---

7 People's reactions to situations vary greatly.

Compare *Night of the Scorpion* (page 18) to one other poem that shows people responding to a situation in which they find themselves.

(27 marks)

---

8 In *Not my Business* (page 42), the poet encourages the reader to think about social responsibility.

Compare this with one other poem that talks about how people relate to each other.

(27 marks)

First Person and Specific Cultural References

On this page you'll find questions on using the <u>first person</u> and <u>specific cultural references</u>. Have a look at pages 60 and 62 for more about these themes. You'll also find lists of appropriate poems that you might want to talk about in your answers.

9 Using the first person to present ideas can have certain advantages.

Compare *Presents from my Aunts...* (page 44) with one other poem in the first person and explain how this device reinforces the poets' ideas.

(27 marks)

10 In *Night of the Scorpion* (page 18), we see the incident through the eyes of a young child.

Find one other poem that uses the first person and compare them.

(27 marks)

11 Some poems portray a certain culture or customs.

Compare *What Were They Like?* (page 22) to one other poem that uses specific cultural references.

(27 marks)

12 Clothes are a specific cultural detail in *Presents from my Aunts...* (page 44).

Find one other poem that uses cultural details and compare how the poets use them.

(27 marks)

Detailed Description and Metaphor

Here are some exam questions on using <u>detailed description</u> and <u>metaphor</u>. Have a look at pages 64 and 66 for more about these themes. You'll also find lists of appropriate poems that you might want to talk about in your answers.

---

13 In *Night of the Scorpion* (page 18) there is detailed description.

Compare how description is used in this poem with how it is used in one other poem.

(27 marks)

---

14 Description is sometimes used to recreate people or places.

Compare the use of description in *Presents from my Aunts...* (page 44) with one other poem.

(27 marks)

---

15 Metaphor is used in *Vultures* (page 20) as a powerful poetic device.

Compare how metaphors are used in *Vultures* and one other poem from the 'Different Cultures' section of the anthology.

(27 marks)

---

16 *Half-Caste* (page 32) uses metaphors to reinforce the poem's message.

Find one other poem that uses metaphors and compare how they emphasise their different subjects.

(27 marks)

Unusual Presentation and Non-Standard English

Now, here are four questions on the use of <u>unusual presentation</u> and <u>non-standard English</u> in poetry. Have a look at pages 68 and 70 for more about these themes and the poems that use them.

---

17 The unusual presentation of a poem often reflects the poet's ideas.

Use *Unrelated Incidents* (page 30) and one other poem to demonstrate how the poets use this technique to support their ideas.

(27 marks)

---

18 Compare the presentation of *What Were They Like?* (page 22) with one other poem which has unusual presentation from the 'Different Cultures' section of the anthology.

(27 marks)

---

19 Language is an important part of our culture.

Limbo (page 4) uses non-standard English to reinforce the ideas in the poem; find another poem that does this and compare them.

(27 marks)

---

20 The way we speak is part of our culture.

Compare the language used in *Unrelated Incidents* (page 30) to one other poem that uses non-standard English.

(27 marks)

Places and Two Cultures

Here are some exam questions on poems about <u>particular places</u> and <u>two different cultures</u>. Have a look at pages 72 and 74 for more about these themes and for lists of the poems that you might want to write about.

21   Some poems, like *Nothing's Changed* (page 8), describe particular places.

      Compare *Nothing's Changed* with one other poem which has a strong sense of place.

(27 marks)

22   *Hurricane Hits England* (page 46) uses a description of a particular place to convey ideas about certain cultures.

      Choose another poem that does this and compare how effective they both are.

(27 marks)

23   Comparing two distinct cultures can provide an effective contrast in a poem, such as in *Island Man* (page 6).

      Compare how the two cultures are used in this and one other poem.

(27 marks)

24   In *Presents from my Aunts...* (page 44), we are presented with a conflict between two cultures.

      Compare how the conflict between two cultures is portrayed in this and one other poem.

(27 marks)

94

Universal Ideas and Traditions

Here's the last lot of practice exam questions. This time, they're on <u>universal ideas</u> and <u>traditions</u>. Look at pages 76 and 78 for more about these themes and the poems that use them.

---

25 Many poets like their work to have universal ideas.

Explain how the poets in *Hurricane Hits England* (page 46) and one other poem present their universal themes.

(27 marks)

---

26 *Vultures* (page 20) examines the universal idea of good and evil.

Choose one other poem and compare how both poems present universal ideas.

(27 marks)

---

27 *Night of the Scorpion* (page 18) describes traditions which are becoming outdated.

Compare this with one other poem which uses the theme of tradition.

(27 marks)

---

28 Traditions are essential ingredients of many cultures.

Show how two poems refer to traditions to make their point. You must use *Presents from my Aunts...* (page 44) as one of your poems.

(27 marks)

Section One — The Poems

A bullet point (•) before an answer means it's just a suggestion — either because there's more than one valid answer, or more than one way of correctly wording the answer.

Page 12 — Limbo

1. • "Knees spread wide" tells you that conditions on the ship were very cramped / uncomfortable because it suggests the ceilings were low.

2. • "burning ground"
   • "sun coming up"
   • "dumb gods are raising me."

3. • The staccato rhythm makes the words sound sharp and harsh. This emphasises the cruelty of the punishment given to the slaves.

4. a) • Repeating these lines reminds us that slave history will always be part of his identity.
   b) • "up / up / up"
   The repetition suggests he is steadily rising out of the misery of slavery.
   The question asks you what the effect is, so you have to work out what impression the poet's trying to create.

5. • One phrase that stands out to me is "long dark night is the silence in front of me". I think this is significant because it sums up how completely empty and hopeless life as a slave must have been.
   You might find it tricky to find an expression that you think really, genuinely stands out from the rest of the poem. If this happens, try thinking about the overall feel of the poem, then find a line that you think sums this feeling up. No one will know you've answered the question backwards.

Page 13 — Island Man

1. Caribbean: "the sound of blue surf" or "emerald island"
   London: "grey metallic soar"

2. "Comes back"
   It's useful if you can spot a phrase like this that links the different bits of a poem together.

3. • The poet creates the impression of being in a dream by using poetic devices, for example in the metaphor "pillow waves". The waves that the man hears are "in his head" rather than in reality.

4. • Having the words "groggily groggily" separated from the rest of the poem emphasises that the man feels like he's somewhere else. Line 14 is also separated, but closer to the rest of the poem, to show that he is gradually returning to reality.

5. • The man probably regrets having to come back to reality. The phrase "heaves himself" suggests he is reluctantly facing up to the dull reality of life in London.

6. • I like the phrase, "the sun surfacing defiantly". It creates a strong, natural image of the man's home island, and makes me feel sorry for him having to live in dreary London.
   It's quite possible you don't really feel sorry for the man. But it's often easier to go along with how the poet is trying to make you feel, rather than trying to come up with something breathtakingly original under the pressure of the exam.

Page 14 — Nothing's Changed

1. • It seems neglected and unkempt. Words like "hard stones", "weeds" and "cans, / trodden on" show the streets are in a poor state of repair.

2. •

	The inn	The cafe
Type of food	haute cuisine	bunny chows
Eating Surface	linen falls	a plastic table's top
Hygiene/cleanliness	crushed ice white glass	spit a little on the floor

3. • These lines suggest that the only difference between South Africa during apartheid and the "new" South Africa is that the segregation is now unofficial.

    Remember to prove to the examiner that you know about the background of the poem.

4. • The poet wants to act violently because he is angry that black and white people are still separated in South Africa. Even though apartheid has been abolished, "Nothing's Changed".

    Poems written in the first person like this one give you a good opportunity to try and see things from the poet's point of view.

5. • The phrase "I press my nose / to the clear panes" stands out to me. I like it because it creates a clear impression of how the poet comes so close to the luxury of the inn, but doesn't feel able to join it because it is founded on discrimination.

Page 15 — Blessing

1. • "god"
    • "congregation"
    • "blessing"

2. a) • "roar of tongues"
    b) • "the blessing sings"

3. • You can tell that water is very precious to the people in the poem because the poet compares it to "silver," which is a valuable substance.

4. • Life seems very desperate for the people. The phrase "Imagine the drip of it" shows us that it has been a long time since the people of the slum have had a dependable water supply.

5. • The items the slum dwellers use to collect the water show us how poor they are. The "pots" and "plastic buckets" sound like items grabbed quickly — it's all they have to collect the water.

    They must be desperate to collect as much water as possible, but all they've got are some pretty inefficient pots and buckets. So even though we're not told outright that they're poor, it's pretty obvious.

6. • I think the phrase "every man woman / child for streets around" is shocking because it shows that many people are thirsty. It really makes me realise how fortunate I am to always have water available.

Page 24 — Two Scavengers in a Truck, Two Beautiful People in a Mercedes

1.

	The Scavengers	The Beautiful People
Their job	garbagemen	his architect's office
Their transport	bright yellow garbage truck	elegant open Mercedes
Their hair	long hair grey iron hair	casually coifed shoulder-length blond hair
Their clothes	red plastic blazers	hip three-piece linen suit short skirt, colored stockings

Look for phrases which emphasise the distance between the rich couple and the poor scavengers — even though they're physically close together at the traffic lights, they're socially far apart.

2. • Any three words from the following: hip, downtown, cool, stoplight, garbagemen, back stoop
    Or other valid answers.

3. • The poem describes a single moment in time. By not using any full stops, the poet emphasises this.

4. • The poet seems to dislike the people in the Mercedes. He describes how wealthy they are with their "elegant open Mercedes" and contrasts this with the "grungy" garbagemen. The poet criticises how unaware the couple seem to be of poverty and inequality in society — they don't even notice the garbagemen. It's like they're in their own privileged world — "an odorless TV ad."

    Remember to quote in questions like this. It shows that your ideas have a basis — you're not just making it up.

Page 25 — Night of the Scorpion

1. a) • "My mother twisted through and through".
    b) • "flash / of diabolic tail"
    The scorpion is also referred to as "the Evil One".

2. • The poet talks about reincarnation, which is a key element of Hinduism.
    You could also mention the holy man's incantation for this question.

3. • I think that using the perspective of a child makes the situation more confusing and frightening.

4. • Telling us that his father is a "sceptic" increases the sense of desperation when even he joins in with the religious response.

5. • The poet seems critical of their response. Near the end he simply says, "it lost its sting", and this seems to imply that it happened quite naturally and had nothing to do with the incantations.

6. • The phrase "giant scorpion shadows" stands out to me. It's a frightening, evil image and it sums up how terrifying the whole experience must have been for the poet as a child.

Page 26 — Vultures

1. •

	The vultures	The Commandant
Ugliness	bashed-in head	hairy / nostrils
Evil	cold / telescopic eyes	fumes of / human roast
Kindness	inclined affectionately	tender offspring

There's loads of descriptive stuff in this poem. These phrases make it nice and easy to compare the vultures and the Commandant.

2. • The phrase "if you will" directly invites the reader to contemplate the issues in the poem.

3. • The poet creates a solemn mood in the poem by using metaphorical language, for example the phrase "greyness / and drizzle of one despondent / dawn" is used to suggest a dark mood. Words like "ogre" and "evil" also create an unpleasant atmosphere.

4. • Both the vultures and the Commandant are disgusting and evil in general, but are still capable of affection — "a tiny glow-worm / tenderness".
    This is the main point of the poem. It might seem like there are two separate bits to the poem, but the stuff about the vultures is there to introduce the idea of human behaviour — so there are loads of parallels.

5. • I find the phrase "they picked / the eyes of a swollen / corpse" really disgusting. It brings home just how horrible the vultures' eating habits are, and this is effective in highlighting how odd it is that they're still capable of tenderness.
    Remember, this poem's meant to be pretty grim. So don't go writing about how beautiful and charming the vultures' eating habits are — you'll just sound twisted.

Page 27 — What Were They Like?

1. • The poem takes a question and answer form. I think that the poet has chosen this form because it appears to be structured and formal. This structure contrasts with the content of the poem, which is emotional and passionate.

2. • "Stone" describes the lanterns that Vietnamese people might have used in Q1, but in A1 it is a metaphor for the people becoming hardened by the war.

3. • The author thinks that the Vietnamese language is delicate and beautiful — "their singing resembled / the flight of moths in moonlight".

4. • The poem suggests that the Vietnamese people lived an idyllic, simple life. We are told that "the water buffalo stepped surely along terraces," which suggests they lived peaceful, unhurried lives.

5. • I find the phrase "after the children were killed," really shocking. It is said in a casual way, which suggests the people responsible for the children's deaths do not think it is very important.

   Remember, there are no wrong answers to this kind of question. But whatever you say, you need to explain why the line you're talking about makes you feel like this.

Page 36 — Search For My Tongue

1. • The poet uses the metaphor of a tree / plant to represent her mother tongue.

2. • She makes you think of her mother tongue as a natural part of her, and one that will always return no matter what she does.

3. • The poet is trying to explain something that is personal to her. She uses "you" and "I" to create an informal, conversational style to express her feelings.

4. • I think this is very important as it lets us appreciate how different Gujarati is to English. This helps to explain why the two tongues are in conflict in the first half of the poem.

   Of course, you could say it's not very important, but it's harder to make a case for that. It's usually easier to say that something's really effective — you can come across as more interested in the poem that way.

5. • I think the phrase "two tongues in your mouth" is effective because it is an unnatural and uncomfortable image. This effectively symbolises the poet's concerns about speaking two languages.

Page 37 — Unrelated Incidents

1. "wanna yoo scruff"

2. a) "You wouldn't think it was true."   b) "There's a right way to spell and a right way to talk."
   c) "You don't know the truth yourselves."

3. • A "BBC accent" means a middle-class, southern English way of speaking.

   The poet refers to it as a "BBC accent" because it's the accent that BBC newsreaders traditionally speak in.

4. • The newsreader says that if the news were read in a regional accent, no one would believe it was the truth — "yi / widny thingk / it wuz troo".

5. • Writing in Scottish dialect allows the poet to use his own natural voice, showing he is not ashamed of it. It also adds humour and irony to the poem.

   Remember, the poet disagrees strongly with the newsreader's view. So he mocks him by 'translating' it into his own dialect. So we hear someone saying that regional accents are inferior, in a regional accent.

6. • The phrase "thirza right / way ti spell" stands out to me because it contradicts itself. The newsreader is saying that variations of English are incorrect, but the poet puts this opinion into Glaswegian dialect. This has a humorous effect, but it also makes the point that people shouldn't dismiss non-standard English as incorrect.

Page 38 — Half-Caste

1. • "when light an shadow / mix in de sky"
   • "england weather / nearly always half-caste"
2. • At the end of the poem the poet says that people must change their attitudes and fully open their eyes, ears and minds before he will tell them everything about himself.
3. • The poet uses humour to make fun of people's attitudes towards mixed-race people. He mocks the term "half-caste" for example by saying he closes "half-a-eye". This is effective because it's a silly and impossible idea.

   You have to show that you can recognise the bits that are meant to be funny, even if they're not exactly like the Two Ronnies. And remember, the jokes aren't just there to try and make you laugh — they're there to show that the poet thinks something is stupid.

4. • The poet uses "I" and "yu" a lot. This allows him to confront the person he is arguing with, e.g. "Explain yuself". Also, his use of dialect allows him to be more direct than if he used standard English grammar.
5. • I find the phrase "half-caste canvas" amusing. Referring to a painting as half-caste sounds peculiar, because it's the mix of colours that makes a painting interesting. The image mocks the idea of referring to people as half-caste.

   What you need to work out in "Half-Caste" is how the stuff about music and painting relates to what he says about being mixed-race.

Page 39 — Love After Love

1. • "Give wine. Give bread."
   • "Feast on your life."
2. • The stranger in the poem is the parts of yourself that get forgotten when you are in a relationship with another person.
3. • The poet suggests that the reader should enjoy their own company: "Give back your heart / To itself". He asks people to celebrate the fact that they are single: "Feast on your life."
4. • The love-letters and photographs are reminders of a life with another person. The poet wants people to remove them so that they can get on with life on their own.
5. • The poet thinks solitary life is a good thing. He says, "Feast on your life," which sounds positive. He suggests that you don't need to be with another person; there's plenty to be had from your own life.
6. • I find the phrase "Give wine. Give bread" reassuring. It makes me think that the poet knows what he's talking about. It also gives the poem a ceremonial feel, suggesting that acceptance of solitary life is an important moment.

   If you can make two or three different points about one particular line, it'll show that you're really thinking about what you're writing. And that can only be a good thing.

Page 48 — This Room

1. • "crash"
   • "bang"
   • "clang"
2. Metaphor: • "the daily furniture of our lives / stirs"
   Effect: • The "daily furniture" represents the routines and habits of everyday life. The poet uses the metaphor as a way of describing the disruption to this routine.

   There's loads of metaphorical language to get stuck into in 'This Room'. Think about why the poet has chosen certain objects to represent how she's feeling, as well as the overall effect of the imagery in the poem.

100

3. • The poet seems happy about what's happening, and she can't quite seem to believe it. She says, "This is the time and place / to be alive", which shows how positive and optimistic she is feeling.

4. • When the room is described as being "in search of space, light, / empty air," this seems to sum up how the poet has been feeling up to this point. I feel happy for the poet, as she has broken free from the uncertainty and boredom she has been feeling.

Page 49 — Not my Business

1. Personification.

2. • The title of the poem is ironic because the activities of the soldiers do become his business when they come to take him away.

    The poet has a clear, strong message in "Not my Business" — he wants people to stand up to the regime.

3. a) • This shows that these incidents are not unusual — they happen regularly.
    b) • This shows that he knows them. It suggests they could be his friends.

4. • These lines show the mindset of someone who ignores what is happening to his neighbours. Repeating them shows that this is an instinctive response — he's not thought it through.

    These lines aren't there in the last verse, because now the person speaking them has become a victim himself.

5. • The phrase "one neat sack for a stainless record" sums up the injustice of life under this brutal regime. It makes me feel angry that Chinwe can be sacked unfairly and get no explanation because it shows that the regime can do whatever they want.

Page 50 — Presents from my Aunts in Pakistan

1. • "conflict"
    • "fractured" • "beggars"

2. a) • I think the phrase means that the poet feels out of place. She doesn't feel like she is at home in England.
    b) • I think the phrase means that the author is trying to 'see herself' wearing the Pakistani clothes. It shows that she is unsure of her identity.

3. • Her memories of Pakistan seem to be vague and uncertain. She mostly relies on second-hand accounts like "photographs" and "newsprint".

4. • The poet feels uncertain of her identity at the end of the poem. The expression "of no fixed nationality" suggests that she doesn't feel fully Pakistani or English.

    The Pakistani clothes make her think about a part of her background that she'd previously ignored.

5. • The poet describes herself as "alien in the sitting-room" when she tries on the Pakistani clothes. This makes me feel sympathy for her, as the clothes make her feel unnatural and out of place, through no fault of her own.

    Remember to try and give a personal response to the poem. Say what your attitude is, or what emotions it makes you feel.

Page 51 — Hurricane Hits England

1. • In Hurricane Hits England the poet lies awake at night listening to a storm. Although the storm is violent, it brings her comfort because it reminds her of the Caribbean where she used to live.

2. The storm that hit England in October 1987.

3. Oya, Huracan and Shango are gods, drawn from African and Mayan mythology.

THE ANSWERS

4. • Before the storm, the poet felt unfulfilled and homesick. She says there was a "frozen lake" inside her, which gives the impression that she was bored and unhappy.

   The first two lines of the poem also suggest this. These clues about how she felt before are important for understanding the storm's effect on her.

5. • At the end of the poem the poet has a different understanding of distance; she realises that everything on Earth is interconnected. This means that she feels less separated from her homeland.

6. • The poet describes the "cratered graves" of the trees. I like this metaphor because it brings home the immense size of the trees that were destroyed, showing the power of the storm.

   If you quote a metaphor the poet's used, make sure you say why you think they've used it, and what effect it has.

Section Two — The Themes

A bullet point (•) before an answer means it's just a suggestion — either because there's more than one valid answer, or more than one way of correctly wording the answer.

Page 53 — Identity

1. • I'm a Scottish girl living in Edinburgh with my dad and brother. I'm fourteen and still at school. I only go to church at Christmas — my family isn't very religious. When I'm older I want to be a gardener — it's what I spend all my spare time doing.

   You don't have to write anything fancy for this question — just show you know the kind of things which make up identity (like your age, gender, ethnic background, religion and interests).

2. • In 'Hurricane Hits England' the poet describes how a woman's identity is linked to where she's from. A woman from the Caribbean is living in England. She doesn't feel at home in England until there's a huge storm, just like the ones they have in the Caribbean. The woman starts to realise that everywhere on Earth is linked: "the earth is the earth is the earth." She finds this liberating; her identity doesn't have to be tied down to one place — she can be at home anywhere.

3. • The poem 'Nothing's Changed' shows how people's identities are to some extent limited and moulded by what other people think of them — and how other people treat them. Under apartheid the man in the poem couldn't have gone to the "whites only inn". Now that apartheid is over though, he is still excluded: "No sign says it is: / but we know where we belong." Because he is poor and classified as non-white the people in that society expect him to continue eating in the "working man's cafe."

   Identity is a big theme that's likely to come up in your exam. It's really useful to do practice questions like these which'll get you thinking about what identity means and how it relates to the poems you're studying.

Page 55 — Political Dimension

1. • I would write a poem about sexism. This issue is important to me because I feel that women are under-represented in many aspects of society — for example, the tiny proportion of female MPs.

   It's worth having a think about what the theme means and how it affects your own life.

2. • In 'What Were They Like?', the poet describes the effects of the Vietnam War. She is very critical of this war. Her descriptions of its devastating effects on Vietnam — "after the children were killed" — leave us in no doubt that she thinks the war was thoughtless and barbaric.

   Make sure you discuss what the poet's attitude is. You won't get many marks just for saying, "This poem is about the Vietnam War" — you have to talk about how the poet uses the descriptions in the poem to make a political point.

3. • 'Nothing's Changed' is about the present-day political situation in South Africa. The poet says that, despite the abolition of apartheid, non-white people are still treated as second-class citizens. He says, "we know where we belong" — he is angry that this inequality still exists.

Page 57 — Change

1. • A big change happened in my life when my family moved house. I had to say goodbye to all my old friends and start a whole new life in the bright lights of Arbroath.

   We all have to face changes throughout our lives. It doesn't have to be something major.

2. • In 'This Room', we witness a dramatic, positive change in the poet's life. We do not know specifically what the change is, but it will clearly affect the poet in a massive way. She rises out of the darkness and limitations she was previously surrounded by, and into enlightenment. The line "my hands are outside, clapping" shows what an incredible moment she is experiencing.

3. • In 'Search For My Tongue', the poet describes a personal change when she dreams in Gujarati. This is a positive change, as she had been worried she had lost her mother tongue — she says it "blossoms out of my mouth".

   "Change" covers a whole range of issues. The change could be good or bad, personal or shared, gradual or sudden.

Page 59 — People

1. • My best friend, Apple, is really important to me. I've known her since I was five. She has always been there for me when I've needed her; she was so supportive when my parents split up.

2. • In 'Vultures', Chinua Achebe creates an evil but complex image of the Commandant. The "fumes of human roast" show that he is a callous murderer, and his "hairy nostrils" make him seem physically repulsive. Yet we are shown that he is still capable of human affection for his child.

3. • In 'Night of the Scorpion', the poet does not interact with the other people very much. He watches the events unfold but does not become involved. The poem starts with "I remember", and from here on he is merely a bewildered spectator of the villagers' reactions to the stinging incident.

   A good way of comparing poems from the 'People' point of view is to look at whether the people in the poems feel like they're part of a group, or as if it's just them against the world.

Page 61 — First Person

1. • Writing in the first person allows the poet to describe their feelings more intensely than if they just used "he" or "she".

   • It makes it easier to argue and persuade people, as the poet can make their point more directly.

2. • In 'Half-Caste', John Agard uses the first person to create an argumentative tone. He repeatedly demands "wha yu mean", which allows him to confront and challenge people who have views he disagrees with.

3. • In 'Presents from my Aunts in Pakistan', I think the poet has chosen to write in the first person because she wants to share her experiences with other people. The first person lets her describe her innermost feelings, e.g. she says she felt "alien in the sitting-room".

   It's easy to spot which poems are written in the first person — it's the ones which have words like "I", "my" and "mine" in them.

Page 63 — Specific Cultural References

1. • I really like the Cornish culture. I went on holiday to Cornwall last summer and we stayed in a quiet, traditional fishing village. The locals were really relaxed and friendly and the food was lovely — stargazy pie every night.

   A lot of the cultures in these poems seem distant and exotic; but remember, there are loads of different cultures and subcultures just within the UK.

2. • In 'Two Scavengers in a Truck...', the poet describes American capitalist culture. He shows that the idea of American democracy is a lie — the "small gulf" between the scavengers and the rich couple in the Mercedes is anything but democratic.

3. • In 'Limbo', Brathwaite develops a strong link to the West Indian slave culture through the metaphor of the limbo dance. He creates a bleak image of slave culture by using phrases like "knees spread wide" to show that there wasn't even enough room to stand up in the ships. This is very important to the poem, as this history is an integral part of the poet's identity.

Page 65 — Description

1. • The funniest thing I've ever seen was our headmistress, falling from the stage in assembly. She landed on the grand piano, which proved unable to support her sizeable frame and promptly collapsed.

    Descriptions can involve personal memories. Look out for when poets do this.

2. • In 'Blessing', the poet's descriptions of the rush to collect water are very effective in creating an idea of how desperate for water the people are. Phrases like "a roar of tongues" and "frantic hands" perfectly describe the sudden, frenzied rush from all corners of the slum.

3. • In 'Island Man', the poet's descriptions of the man suggest that she feels sorry for him. For example, she describes him returning to reality, "groggily groggily", making him sound tired and confused. He reluctantly "heaves himself" up, and this description shows the poet feels sympathy for him because he'd clearly much rather stay in bed dreaming of his home.

    Many poets show how they feel through the adjectives and metaphors they use, rather than stating their opinions outright.

Page 67 — Metaphor

1. • Poets can use metaphors to express just how strongly they feel about something or someone. They can be more effective than ordinary, literal descriptions because they help to create an image in the reader's mind.

    In short, metaphors make a poem sound a bit more interesting.

2. • In 'Half-Caste' the poet uses metaphors to mock the description of people as "half-caste". He uses a metaphor to compare himself to a painting that mixes "red an green". This ridicules the idea that the colour of his skin makes him an incomplete person since mixing colours in a painting makes it even more detailed and complete.

3. • In 'Search For My Tongue', Sujata Bhatt uses metaphors to create the impression that languages are alive like a plant. She is worried that her mother tongue will "rot and die". This becomes a running metaphor — she says "it blossoms out of my mouth" when she realises that she dreams in Gujarati.

    A running metaphor is when the poet keeps on going with the same metaphor, using different aspects of the image. They're also called extended metaphors.

Page 69 — Unusual Presentation

1. • A poet might use an unusual style of presentation to create a particular visual effect. This could be to reflect the poem's theme.

2. • In 'Search For My Tongue', part of the poem is written in Gujarati script. This makes it clear how different Gujarati looks and sounds compared to English, which helps to explain why the poet's mother tongue is so important to her identity.

    If a poem's set out on the page in an odd way, it's not only to make it stand out. There'll be a specific reason why it looks like that — usually related to the poem's theme.

3. • In 'Unrelated Incidents', the short lines and lack of punctuation make the poem look like a newsreader's autocue. This humorously reflects the poem's theme of the perceived attitude of a BBC newsreader.

Page 71 — Non-Standard English

1. • Non-standard English means any form of English that is different from standard forms of grammar and pronunciation.

   Standard English accents are sometimes called 'received pronunciation', or 'the Queen's English'.

2. • In 'Limbo', the poet uses simplified forms of grammar related to West Indian Creole, e.g. "stick hit sound". He does this to emphasise the connection he feels with the Caribbean slaves.

3. • In 'Unrelated Incidents', the style of language is crucial to the poem's impact. The theme of the poem is people's attitudes towards regional accents. By using expressions like "yi canny talk / right", the poet mocks the views of those who see accents as inferior.

   In 'Unrelated Incidents', the whole poem is written in dialect. Look out for poems like 'Half-Caste', where the non-standard dialect is mixed in with standard English.

Page 73 — Particular Places

1. • My favourite place is Morecambe. It's got a big, old-fashioned sea front which is alive with the sounds of seagulls and holiday-makers. It's a vibrant, exciting place which always brings back memories.

2. • In 'Nothing's Changed', the descriptions of District Six make it seem wild and neglected. "Small round hard stones" create a harsh feel, and the grasses and seeds suggest the streets are being reclaimed by nature.

   The physical appearance of District Six is important because it's symbolic of the poet's opinion that nothing has been done to improve black people's lives.

3. • In 'Two Scavengers in a Truck...', the setting is important because the poem is about American society specifically. Phrases like "nine a.m. downtown San Francisco" show that what is described in the poem is a normal, everyday situation.

Page 75 — Two Cultures

1. • I feel that I belong to just one culture. I have lived in Bradford all my life, and although my father is Welsh, I have never been to Wales — I feel Yorkshire through and through.

   Lots of the poems in this anthology deal with cultures from the point of view of how they affect the poet's sense of identity. Some, though, are more political, e.g. 'Unrelated Incidents'.

2. • In 'Search For My Tongue', the poet feels that the two cultures cannot mix. The two cultures in her life are represented by languages. She says that her mother tongue "could not really know the other", suggesting that they will always be separate, conflicting parts of her identity.

3. • In 'Half-Caste', John Agard says that it's a good thing when different cultures mix together. He says that, to make classical music, you "mix a black key / wid a white key" — this metaphor suggests that mixing different components together can have a creative effect.

   With the 'Two Cultures' theme, the poems generally fall into one of two camps — some say cultures can mix together, others say they clash. Picking one of each and then comparing them is a good idea for the exam questions.

Page 77 — Universal Ideas

1. • Last week I saw 'The Day After Tomorrow'. The film really made me think about the issues surrounding global warming because it could change the world forever. I've decided that I'm going to make more journeys on my bike instead of asking my dad for a lift so I make a little contribution to reducing greenhouse gas emissions.

2. • The theme in 'Love After Love' is solitary life. The poet presents it as a positive thing, by using words like "elation". Because there are no specific details given, like names or places, the poet's advice seems to apply to anyone at any time.

3. • In 'Vultures', the vultures are seen as disgusting yet affectionate. This is related to the idea of good and evil in people when they are linked to the Commandant, who is a murderer but loves his child. The poet links these examples together with the word "Thus", showing that they demonstrate the same theme.

   Some poets have a strong opinion and try to convince you that they're right, e.g. 'Half-Caste'. Others are less certain, and just want to get people thinking about an issue, like in 'Vultures'.

Page 79 — Traditions

1. • Every summer after the last day of school, my friend Junior and I go and play pooh sticks from the bridge by the park in our village. We've done this every year for as long as I can remember.

2. • In 'What Were They Like?', the poet creates a mysterious but beautiful impression of Vietnamese traditions. Although there is an uncertain tone, the suggestion of holding "ceremonies / to reverence the opening of buds" hints at an ancient, respectful set of traditions.

3. • In 'Hurricane Hits England', the poet calls on African and Mayan storm gods to explain the severe weather. This shows how strong her connection with her homeland in the Caribbean is, explaining why she is homesick. This adds to the impact when she realises that 'the earth is the earth is the earth'.

Marking the Exam-Style Questions

There aren't any detailed answers to the exam-style questions here because there are loads of possible answers that would be equally valid. Instead, we've included plenty of bullet points that give you an idea of the points you could make in your essay. If you want a bit more guidance, have another look at the sample essays and notes on pages 80-87.

This list tells you all the things you need to do to get a grade A or above in an exam essay.
Read it carefully and try to do as many of these things as you can in your answers to the exam-style questions. Then, when you've finished an answer, go back to this list and check how many of the things you've managed to do. If you've missed any out, then make an effort to include them in your next essay.

> • Read the questions carefully and jot down some notes to plan your answer. When you start writing, make sure that you stick to answering the question — don't start waffling about stuff that just isn't relevant.
>
> • Use quotations in your answer to back up every point you make.
>   The quotations have to be worked into your sentences, not just stuck on the end.
>
> • Pick out lots of different writing techniques used by the writer. As well as knowing what the methods are you need to explain why they've been chosen and what effect they're supposed to have on the reader.
>
> • Show that you appreciate what the author's thoughts and feelings about a particular issue are.
>   You need to be able to relate this to your own views and experiences.
>
> • Pay particular attention to the characters in the poem — you have to be able to show that you understand how the poet presents people.
>
> • Mention the structure of the poem, especially if the presentation is unusual. You have to be able to discuss what effect the presentation of the poem has and how well you think it works.
>
> • When you compare two poems, you have to write about both of them throughout your answer. You can't just write half an essay about one poem and then half about the other; you've got to keep discussing and comparing them both as you go along.
>
> • Finally, don't forget the basics. Make sure that your handwriting is neat — you won't get any marks if they can't read what you've written. Also, pay attention to your spelling, grammar and punctuation.

If you're hoping to get an A*, you have to do all the things in the list above with confidence.
You also need to show some originality and flair in your answers.
This means that you've got to be imaginative and show the examiner that you have understood the poems in lots of detail and that you've got something interesting to say about them.

1. For this question, you must compare ideas about identity in *Nothing's Changed* with <u>one</u> other poem from the anthology. *Limbo, Island Man, Half Caste, Love After Love, This Room, Search For My Tongue, Hurricane Hits England, Presents from my Aunts in Pakistan* and *Unrelated Incidents* are all about identity. I've picked *Presents from my Aunts in Pakistan*. You only have 45 minutes to answer the question so just include a short introduction and conclusion and concentrate on comparing the poems. The most important thing to remember is to compare the poems. Don't just talk about one poem and then the other — you have to say how they're similar and different. Here are some points you could include in your answer:

    • In *Nothing's Changed*, the poet comments on his own identity through his discussion of the segregation that still exists in post-apartheid South Africa. He describes his physical recognition of the place he once knew, and once felt at home in, through the words "my feet know".

    • The poet reflects on the racial inequality that still exists, and on his own place within the segregated society, in the phrase "No sign says it is: / but we know where we belong".

    • He shows that he's an outsider to the life of luxury that white people in South Africa experience. The phrase "I press my nose / to the clear panes" shows that he can only look at, but can't join in with, their luxuries.

    • He shows that black and mixed-race people in South Africa, including himself, have experienced inequality for so long that it just feels normal. He says, "it's in the bone".

    • He shows that he's angry about the identity that's been imposed on non-whites because of their race. The phrase "Hands burn" shows this anger and shows that he wants to take action against the inequality.

    • In *Presents from my Aunts*, the poet describes her mixed feelings about presents she receives from Pakistan, which reflect her feelings about her own identity.

    • She is unsure of her identity and feels like she's "of no fixed nationality" because she's "half-English". This contrasts with the poet of *Nothing's Changed*, who is perfectly sure of his identity, but is unhappy because of the way others see him and treat him.

    • She describes how beautiful the presents are — "glistening like an orange split open", but says they make her feel "alien" and that she "could never be as lovely / as those clothes".

    • She's more comfortable with plain Western clothes like "denim and corduroy" and says that her Pakistani clothes "didn't impress the schoolfriend". She wants to fit in with her English friends.

    • The Pakistani clothes make her think about her journey to England and her birthplace in Pakistan. She pictures herself "staring through fretwork", as though there's a barrier stopping her from being a part of Pakistan. This is similar to the part of *Nothing's Changed* where the poet stares through glass at the white people's luxury. He's also separated from others because of his identity.

    • The poet describes times when the two cultures of her identity clashed, such as when her mum's jewellery was "stolen from our car". This represents her own internal struggle with her two cultures. This contrasts with *Nothing's Changed* where two types of people are kept separate from each other — when most of them had no choice about the type of person they were labelled as.

2. For this question, you must compare ideas about identity in *Love After Love* with <u>one</u> other poem from the anthology. *Limbo, Island Man, Half Caste, Love After Love, This Room, Search For My Tongue, Hurricane Hits England, Presents from my Aunts in Pakistan, Nothing's Changed* and *Unrelated Incidents* are all about identity. I've picked *Hurricane Hits England*. You only have 45 minutes to answer the question so just include a short introduction and conclusion and concentrate on comparing the poems. The most important thing to remember is to compare the poems. Don't just talk about one poem and then the other — you have to say how they're similar and different. Here are some points you could include in your answer:

    • In *Love After Love*, the poet describes discovering your own identity and learning to love yourself at the end of a relationship. He writes in the form of instructions, such as "Feast on your life".

    • The poet says you will discover your own identity with "elation". He states that "The time will come" as though what he is saying is definite and assured — this makes him sound very confident.

    • He talks about discovering yourself as though returning to someone abandoned, with "You will love again the stranger who was your self". The self is described as a person who has remained loyal through hard times and betrayal.

    • References to other lovers are quite bitter and negative. The poet encourages us to "Take down the love-letters" and forget about past loves because loving another person means you neglect yourself and forget your own identity.

• In *Hurricane Hits England*, the poet experiences a massive storm at her home in England. It makes her think of her childhood home in the Caribbean where hurricanes were common, and she realises that the two places are not so different after all. It makes her feel more at home in England. In this poem, identity is explored in terms of cultural roots, in comparison to *Love After Love* where identity is never defined except as something you will be happier about in the future.

• She describes the storm as "some dark ancestral spectre", as it brings back memories of the beliefs of African and Mayan people about scary, but well-meaning, storm gods. She feels a sudden spiritual connection to her ancestral roots, which she describes as "Fearful and reassuring".

• She addresses the storm gods in a friendly way: "Talk to me Huracan", and describes a hurricane from her childhood as her "sweeping, back-home cousin". The weather is comforting to her, like a family member.

• The poet asks, "O why is my heart unchained?", which means she may feel suddenly free from the restraints of England, and instead connected to her homeland. This is similar to the way in which the poet of *Love After Love* describes becoming free from a previous lover and getting to know yourself again.

• The poet uses a metaphor which connects the effects of the storm to her own feelings: "Shaking the foundations of the very trees within me". This shows that her own cultural 'roots' have been shaken out and revealed and that she feels liberated and happier about herself.

• The final line suggests she no longer feels homesick, as she realises that "the earth is the earth is the earth". This is similar to the confident, calm way in which the poet of *Love After Love* describes the comfort gained from getting to know your true inner self.

3. For this question, you must compare ideas about politics in *Two Scavengers in a Truck...* with <u>one</u> other poem from the anthology. *Not my Business, Nothing's Changed, Vultures, What Were They Like?* and *Unrelated Incidents* are all about politics. I've picked *What Were They Like?* You only have 45 minutes to answer the question so just include a short introduction and conclusion and concentrate on comparing the poems. The most important thing to remember is to compare the poems. Don't just talk about one poem and then the other — you have to say how they're similar and different. Here are some points you could include in your answer:

• *Two Scavengers in a Truck...* describes the stark contrast between rich and poor in American society. The poet compares "two garbagemen in red plastic blazers" with "an elegant couple" in "an elegant open Mercedes".

• The garbagemen are described as "gazing down / as from a great distance" at the elegant couple as though "watching some odorless TV ad". This suggests that the garbagemen long to live like the rich couple, but it's just a fantasy, not a possibility.

• While the garbagemen stare at them, the rich couple haven't noticed the garbagemen — they are unaware and unconcerned about the contrast in society.

• The poet describes similarities between two of the people. The younger garbageman is "about the same age as the Mercedes driver" and they both have longish hair and sunglasses. However, these similarities are only superficial — their lives are so different that they would never be friends.

• The poet uses the distance between the two couples at the stop light to represent the difference between rich and poor. He describes it as a "small gulf / in the high seas / of this democracy". He is implying that although the gap is small, it's impossible to cross, which shouldn't be the case in a democracy where everyone is supposed to have an equal say.

• *What Were They Like?* is another poem with a political message. In this case, it is about the effect of the Vietnam War on the people of Vietnam.

• The poem is presented in the style of a formal military report, which sounds impersonal and unemotional on the surface with phrases such as "Sir" and "It is not remembered". However, some shocking emotional topics are covered using this tone, as in the phrase "after the children were killed". The poet feels that the American government was unconcerned about destroying the lives of normal Vietnamese people. Similarly, the American government is criticised in *Two Scavengers...* for failing to be concerned about the divide between rich and poor.

• The poet shows how the Vietnam War destroyed the culture and way of life of ordinary Vietnamese people. We are told that they had "light hearts" and that they were "peasants" leading peaceful lives. The war destroyed all this and now "laughter is bitter to the burned mouth". The language used to show the destruction is more powerful than in *Two Scavengers...* — this is a bitter and regretful criticism of the government rather than the mildly cynical criticism in *Two Scavengers...*

• The poem describes the Vietnamese people as though they are a long-extinct culture that cannot be remembered properly. Phrases such as "It is silent now" show us that their culture could be lost for ever as a result of the Vietnam War. This creates a very sad and emotional image, in comparison to the potentially humorous images of gargoyles and "odorless" TV ads in *Two Scavengers*…

4. For this question, you must compare ideas about politics in *Not my Business* with <u>one</u> other poem from the anthology. *Nothing's Changed, Vultures, What Were They Like?, Two Scavengers in a Truck*… and *Unrelated Incidents* are all about politics. I've picked *Nothing's Changed*. You only have 45 minutes to answer the question so just include a short introduction and conclusion and concentrate on comparing the poems. The most important thing to remember is to compare the poems. Don't just talk about one poem and then the other — you have to say how they're similar and different. Here are some points you could include in your answer:
    *   *Not my Business* is a poem about the mistreatment of people in an African country. The narrator of the poem turns a blind eye until he himself is taken away. The message of the poem is that people should stand up against oppressive regimes.
    *   The narrator of the poem describes how his friend is taken away by some people in a jeep who "Beat him soft like clay". The narrator's reaction is, "What business of mine is it / So long they don't take the yam / From my savouring mouth?" He ignores the brutality of the regime simply because he's not directly affected by it.
    *   Although the narrator ignores the oppressive regime, the poet is angry about it. You can tell this by the way he describes the abuse, for example "No query, no warning, no probe" about the sacking of a friend.
    *   Phrases such as "one night" make the incidents sound as though they're common occurrences, inevitable and normal to everyone. This contrasts with the time when "The jeep" comes for the narrator. Now, he describes the incident with emotion and fear as "A knock on the door froze my hungry hand". Only when he's affected does he feel emotional about the abuse.
    *   *Nothing's Changed* is also about an unfair regime in an African country. This time, however, the problem is to do with inequalities and mistreatment in society caused by the government's regime, rather than to do with actual physical abuse.
    *   The poet reflects on the racial inequality that still exists in post-apartheid South Africa, and on his own place within society in the phrase "No sign says it: / but we know where we belong".
    *   He shows that he's an outsider to the life of luxury that white people in South Africa experience. The phrase "I press my nose / to the clear panes" shows that he can look at, but doesn't feel he can join in with, their luxuries.
    *   He shows that black and 'coloured' people in South Africa, including himself, have experienced inequality for so long that it just feels normal. He says, "it's in the bone". This is similar to the situation described in *Not my Business* — people have just got used to the regime and it feels normal and not something to protest about.
    *   The poet shows that he's angry about the segregation that still exists as a result of apartheid. The phrase "Hands burn" shows this anger and shows that he wants to take action against the inequality. The poet in *Not my Business* feels the same way about the oppressive regime, but he expresses it differently through the example of a man who says "What business of mine is it…?" until he too becomes personally involved.

5. For this question, you must compare ideas about change in *Search For My Tongue* with <u>one</u> other poem from the anthology. *Blessing, Love After Love, Hurricane Hits England, Nothing's Changed, What Were They Like?, Presents from my Aunts*… and *This Room* are all about change. I've picked *Presents from my Aunts*…. You only have 45 minutes to answer the question so just include a short introduction and conclusion and concentrate on comparing the poems. Don't just talk about one poem and then the other — you have to say how they're similar and different. Here are some points you could include in your answer:
    *   In *Search For My Tongue*, the poet talks about change when she describes how she's worried that she's forgotten her first language. She is then pleased when it returns in her dreams.
    *   The poet has experienced change in her life once already — she originally lived in India, but now lives in another country and has had to learn a "foreign tongue".
    *   She finds it hard to have "two tongues in your mouth" — she can't use them both together, "even if you thought that way".
    *   She worries that if she only uses the "foreign tongue", the "mother tongue would rot". This is a sickening image, which shows that she feels as though forgetting her native language would be as awful a change as losing a part of her body.
    *   Later in the poem, she shows that her mother tongue returns while she dreams – "it grows back, a stump of a shoot" and eventually "it blossoms out of my mouth". The plant metaphor makes the tongue sound like a part of nature — something that has a life of its own. She's happy with the realisation that her mother tongue will always be a part of her — that she hasn't lost it after all.

- In *Presents from my Aunts....*, a similar change is being explored. The poet also moved from one country to another at an early age and had to adapt to her new culture. She describes receiving beautiful presents from her aunts in Pakistan and trying them on, but feeling "alien" in them. This leads her to comment on how, being "half-English", she doesn't know where she belongs.
- In contrast to *Search For My Tongue*, the poet never really felt like a full part of Pakistan, and so is less worried about 'losing' her links to her native country than deciding which country she really belongs in. She comments on the "cruelty / and the transformation" of a camel into a "camel-skin lamp" as a metaphor for the change in her own life in terms of her culture and identity.
- Just as the dream in *Search For My Tongue* brings back her native language, the presents in *Presents from my Aunts…* bring back the poet's imagined memories of herself in Pakistan. However, this doesn't make her happy or comforted; it makes her more insecure about being "of no fixed nationality".
- The change in this poem, the move from Pakistan to England, brings the poet emotional pain because she can't remember it properly. She says "I pictured my birthplace / from fifties' photographs" and read about troubles in Pakistan "through newsprint". If she'd known more about her birthplace, her problems might be more like those in *Search For My Tongue*, worrying about forgetting her homeland.

6. For this question, you must compare ideas about change in *What Were They Like?* with one other poem from the anthology. *Blessing, Love After Love, Hurricane Hits England, Nothing's Changed, Search For My Tongue, Presents from my aunts…* and *This Room* are all about change. I've picked *Nothing's Changed*. You only have 45 minutes to answer the question so just include a short introduction and conclusion and concentrate on comparing the poems. The most important thing to remember is to compare the poems. Don't just talk about one poem and then the other — you have to say how they're similar and different. Here are some points you could include in your answer:
- *What Were They Like?* is a poem about the effect of the Vietnam War on the people of Vietnam. It describes how the Vietnamese people were peaceful, happy people who lived simple lives farming. It then explains how their history and culture has been brutally and shockingly destroyed.
- The poem is presented in the style of a formal military report, which sounds impersonal and unemotional on the surface with phrases such as "Sir" and "It is not remembered". However, some shocking emotional topics are covered using this tone, as in the phrase "after the children were killed". This makes the effects of the war seem even more barbaric and appalling.
- The poet shows how the Vietnam War destroyed the culture and way of life of ordinary Vietnamese people. We are told that they had "light hearts" and that they were "peasants" leading peaceful lives. The war destroyed all this and now "laughter is bitter to the burned mouth". The harsh alliteration in phrases such as this reinforces the horror of the napalm bombing.
- The poem describes the Vietnamese people as though they are a long-extinct culture that cannot be remembered properly. Phrases such as "It is silent now" show us that their culture could be lost forever as a result of the Vietnam War. This creates a very sad and emotional image.
- *Nothing's Changed* is about the segregation that still exists in post-apartheid South Africa. The poet returns to "District Six" where he used to live and describes the segregation that is still obvious there, even after the end of apartheid. He makes the point that despite expectations, nothing really has changed after all.
- The poet reflects on his own place within society in the phrase "No sign says it is: but we know where we belong". He shows that he's an outsider to the life of luxury that white people in South Africa experience. The phrase "I press my nose / to the clear panes" shows that he can only look at, but doesn't feel he can join in with, their luxuries. He is angry about this because apartheid is over and people of all races should be able to mix freely.
- The poet says he is reminded of being a child in the phrase "boy again". Memories of the past are negative for him and he's angry that nothing has changed. This contrasts starkly with memories of the past in *What Were They Like?* where the past was a wonderful, happy, peaceful time.
- He shows that black and mixed-race people in South Africa, including himself, have experienced inequality for so long that it just feels normal. He says, "it's in the bone". This is very different from the feelings expressed in *What Were They Like?* where people's lives have so dramatically changed for the worse. The lives of Vietnamese people will never be the same again and it will take them a long time to adapt.
- The poet shows that he's angry about the segregation that still exists as a result of apartheid. The phrase "Hands burn" shows this anger and he looks for a stone to "shiver down the glass" showing that he wants to take action against the inequality. The poet of *What Were They Like?* feels angry too, but there's nothing she can do to change things for the better in Vietnam.

7. For this question, you must compare people's reactions in *Night of the Scorpion* with <u>one</u> other poem from the anthology. *Half-Caste, Vultures, Search For My Tongue, Presents from my Aunts...Not my Business, Two Scavengers...., Island Man* and *Hurricane Hits England* all include ideas about people's reactions to situations. I've picked *Hurricane Hits England*. You only have 45 minutes to answer the question so just include a short introduction and conclusion and concentrate on comparing the poems. The most important thing to remember is to compare the poems. Don't just talk about one poem and then the other — you have to say how they're similar and different. Here are some points you could include in your answer:
    *   *Night of the Scorpion* is the poet's recollection of when his mother was stung by a scorpion. He describes the reactions of local people and the actions of a holy man. It's terrifying for a small boy.
    *   The villagers who come to watch are described as "swarms of flies". This shows how panic-stricken and illogical their reactions were, and how they made it all the more scary for the poet.
    *   The villagers begin to chant phrases that sound like prayers, such as "May the sins of your previous birth / be burned away tonight". The poet describes this through repetitive phrases which make their reaction seem unthinking. The chanting is about reincarnation, suggesting that they think she'll die tonight. This adds to the fear and uncertainty.
    *   In comparison to the reaction of the villagers, the poet's father is "sceptic, rationalist". He tries "every curse and blessing, / powder, mixture, herb and hybrid" in the hope that something will work. His reactions are more practical, but possibly equally panic-stricken as the villagers' reactions.
    *   The "holy man" performed "his rites". The poet describes this in a slightly ironic way, saying that he tries to "tame the poison with an incantation". This suggests he knows the holy man's actions are pointless.
    *   His mother is the only person who has been calm throughout. She "only said / Thank God the scorpion picked on me / and spared my children."
    *   The poet's description of events is presented in a matter-of-fact tone, suggesting he now realises that the outcome was inevitable and the panic was unnecessary, for example "After twenty hours / it lost its sting". This tone also shows how he is just an observer throughout and is powerless to help.
    *   In *Hurricane Hits England*, the poet experiences a massive storm at her home in England. It makes her think of her childhood home in the Caribbean where hurricanes were common, and she realises that the two places are not so different after all. It makes her feel more at home in England.
    *   She describes the storm as "some dark ancestral spectre", as it brings back memories of the beliefs of African and Mayan people about scary, but well-meaning, storm gods. She feels a sudden spiritual connection to her ancestral roots, which she describes as "Fearful and reassuring".
    *   She addresses the storm gods in a friendly way: "Talk to me Huracan", and describes a hurricane from her childhood as her "sweeping, back-home cousin". The weather is comforting to her, like a family member, which is surprising considering it's a powerful and frightening storm. This contrasts with the panic described in *Night of the Scorpion* – the poet of *Hurricane Hits England* is very calm and reflective.
    *   The poet uses a metaphor which connects the effects of the storm to her own feelings: "Shaking the foundations of the very trees within me". This shows that her own cultural 'roots' have been shaken out and revealed and that she feels liberated and happier about herself. She gains a great insight from her eventful night, compared to *Night of the Scorpion*, where the poet only discovers that all the panic was pointless.
    *   The final line suggests she no longer feels homesick, as she realises that "the earth is the earth is the earth". This is similar to the calm way in which the poet of *Night of the Scorpion* concludes his poem with his mother's calm and unselfish reaction.

8. For this question, you must compare how people relate to each other in *Not my Business* with <u>one</u> other poem from the anthology. *Half-Caste, Night of the Scorpion, Two Scavengers...* and *Nothing's Changed* all include ideas about how people relate to each other. I've picked *Two Scavengers....* You only have 45 minutes to answer the question so just include a short introduction and conclusion and concentrate on comparing the poems. The most important thing to remember is to compare the poems. Don't just talk about one poem and then the other — you have to say how they're similar and different. Here are some points you could include in your answer:
    *   *Not my Business* is a poem about the mistreatment of people through an oppressive regime in an African country. The narrator of the poem turns a blind eye until he himself is taken away. The message of the poem is that people should stand up against brutal regimes.
    *   The narrator of the poem describes how his friend is taken away by some people in a jeep who "Beat him soft like clay". The narrator's reaction is, "What business of mine is it / So long they don't take the yam / From my savouring mouth?" He ignores the brutality of the regime simply because he's not directly affected by it.

- Although the narrator ignores the oppressive regime, the poet is angry about it. You can tell this by the way he describes the abuse, for example "No query, no warning, no probe" about the sacking of a friend.
- Phrases such as "one night" make the incidents sound as though they're common occurrences, inevitable and normal to everyone. This contrasts with the time when "The jeep" comes for the narrator. Now, he describes the incident with emotion and fear as "A knock on the door froze my hungry hand". Only when he's affected does he feel emotional about the abuse.
- *Two Scavengers...* compares "two garbagemen in red plastic blazers" with "an elegant couple" in "an elegant open Mercedes". The poem has a political message about the difference between rich and poor in "this democracy".
- The garbagemen are described as "gazing down / as from a great distance" at the elegant couple as though "watching some odorless TV ad". This suggests that the garbagemen long to live like the rich couple, but it's just a fantasy, not a possibility.
- While the garbagemen stare at them, the rich couple haven't noticed the garbagemen — they are unaware and unconcerned about the lives of people like the garbagemen. This is a similar attitude to the narrator in *Not my Business* — he too is unconcerned about issues in society as long as he isn't affected and he gets his "yam".
- The poet describes similarities between two of the people. The younger garbageman is "about the same age as the Mercedes driver" and they both have longish hair and sunglasses. However, these similarities are only superficial — their lives are so different that they would never be friends and have no reason to be concerned about each other's lives. This contrasts with the relationships in *Not my Business*, where the narrator's friends are affected by the brutal regime, but he still ignores what's going on.

9. For this question, you must compare the use of the first person in *Presents from my Aunts...* with <u>one</u> other poem from the anthology. *Limbo, Half-Caste, Hurricane Hits England, Search For My Tongue, This Room, Nothing's Changed, Not my Business* and *Night of the Scorpion* are all written in the first person. I've picked *This Room*. You only have 45 minutes to answer the question so just include a short introduction and conclusion and concentrate on comparing the poems. The most important thing to remember is to compare the poems. Don't just talk about one poem and then the other — you have to say how they're similar and different. Here are some points you could include in your answer:
- In *Presents from my Aunts...*, the poet describes her mixed feelings about presents she receives from Pakistan, which reflect her feelings about her own identity. She uses the first person throughout to explain her feelings and personal reactions.
- She is unsure of her identity and feels like she's "of no fixed nationality" because she's "half-English".
- She describes how beautiful the presents are — "glistening like an orange split open", but says they make her feel "alien" and that she "could never be as lovely / as those clothes". This is a very personal reaction to the clothes.
- She's more comfortable with plain Western clothes like "denim and corduroy" and says that her Pakistani clothes "didn't impress the schoolfriend". She wants to fit in with her English friends.
- The use of the first person allows her to make simple, direct statements, such as "I wanted" and "I longed / for". These statements show how sure she is about her own feelings, and how confident she is to discuss them, despite being confused about her identity.
- *This Room* is a poem which describes feelings of elation about something, although we don't know what. The elation is expressed through the personification of the room, which "is breaking out / of itself", with all the furniture lifting up and flying around the room.
- The first person is only used in the last four lines, compared to *Presents from my Aunts...* which uses it throughout. The previous lines are a description of the activities of the room, for example "Pots and pans bang together". It is only in the last few lines that you realise the previous description has been one big metaphor to express the poet's feelings of elation.
- When the first person is used and the poem becomes specific to the poet personally, there is still a sense of unconnectedness. Rather than explaining her thoughts and feelings explicitly, as the poet of *Presents from my Aunts...* does, she says, "I've left my feet" and "my hands are outside" as though she has no control over herself in all the excitement.
- The effect of not using the first person throughout most of this poem is that it enhances the feeling of bewilderment, and creates an effect of excited confusion.

10. For this question, you must compare the use of the first person in *Night of the Scorpion* with <u>one</u> other poem from the anthology. *Limbo, Half-Caste, Hurricane Hits England, Search For My Tongue, This Room, Nothing's Changed, Not my Business* and *Presents from my Aunts…* are all written in the first person. I've picked *Search For My Tongue*. You only have 45 minutes to answer the question so just include a short introduction and conclusion and concentrate on comparing the poems. The most important thing to remember is to compare the poems. Don't just talk about one poem and then the other — you have to say how they're similar and different. Here are some points you could include in your answer:

• *Night of the Scorpion* is the poet's recollection of being a young boy and watching his mother suffering after being stung by a scorpion. He describes the panicked reactions of the villagers and his father.

• The poem starts with "I remember", which shows from the beginning that the poem is written in the first person and is a personal account.

• The poet writes, "I watched the flame feeding on my mother", which is a horrific image, and a terrifying experience for a young child. The fact that he starts with "I watched" shows that he feels powerless to help. All he can do is watch while his mother writhes in pain.

• The poet describes some events from a childish perspective, as he would have experienced them at the time; for example, he describes "giant scorpion shadows". However, he also describes some events with the wisdom of age. For example, he says, "After twenty hours / it lost its sting", as though it was obvious that this would happen, which he wouldn't have known as a child.

• The effect of this poem being written in the first person is that the reader can empathise with the small boy. The line "My mother twisted through and through" gives the reader a strong idea of the fear and confusion that the child would be experiencing.

• *Search For My Tongue* is also written in the first person. It is about the poet's fear that she has forgotten her native language. The fear is overcome because her "mother tongue" returns to her in her dreams.

• The first person is used in this poem to create a conversational tone. The poet addresses the reader as "you" to get them more involved in her issues. For example, the first line is "You ask me what I mean", which implies that a conversation has already begun.

• The poet gets the reader personally involved by asking what "you" would do in her situation "if you had two tongues in your mouth". This contrasts with *Night of the Scorpion*, which is simply an account from the poet's childhood. He asks for no reassurance or involvement from the reader.

• Later in the poem she describes how her mother tongue "grows longer" and "ties the other tongue in knots". She's happy that her mother tongue is as strong as ever, but describes it as though it's something separate from her that she has no control of. This is similar to the events being described in *Night of the Scorpion* — the poet describes an event that he has no control over.

• Both poems use the first person effectively to allow the reader to understand their complex personal emotions.

11. For this question, you must compare specific cultural references in *What Were They Like?* with <u>one</u> other poem from the anthology. *Two Scavengers…, Nothing's Changed, Limbo, Night of the Scorpion* and *Hurricane Hits England* all contain specific cultural references. I've picked *Limbo*. You only have 45 minutes to answer the question so just include a short introduction and conclusion and concentrate on comparing the poems. The most important thing to remember is to compare the poems. Don't just talk about one poem and then the other — you have to say how they're similar and different. Here are some points you could include in your answer:

• *What Were They Like?* is written in the style of a military report about the effect of the Vietnam War on the ordinary people of Vietnam.

• In the poem we learn that most Vietnamese people "were peasants; their life / was in rice and bamboo". This shows that they lived simple, peaceful lives, which makes the war seem even more barbaric.

• The poem also makes references to their speech and songs. It says, "their speech which was like a song" and "their singing resembled / the flight of moths in moonlight", which suggest the soft, gentle beauty of their language and culture. However, this culture seems lost forever because of the war as the poem concludes with "It is silent now".

• The Vietnamese people are also seen as nature-loving and peaceful — "they gathered once to delight in blossom". This is contrasted with the effects of the war — "after the children were killed / there were no more buds".

• References to the culture of the Vietnamese people are cautious and vague, using words such as "perhaps". There are also lots of instances of uncertainty, such as "It is not remembered". This makes their culture sound as though it is long-forgotten and lost for ever.

• The poem *Limbo* also contains strong cultural references. It is about the journey of slaves from Africa on slave ships, with references to the traditional dance they brought with them.

• The conditions the slaves faced on the ship are described in the line "long dark night is the silence in front of me". This reference to the experiences of the slaves is much more vague and subject to interpretation than references to the lives of Vietnamese people in *What Were They Like?* where references are straightforward, such as "stone lanterns illumined pleasant ways".

• The cruelty and beatings the slaves faced are described in the lines "stick is the whip" and "stick hit sound". These lines are also linked to the "stick" in the limbo dance.

• The limbo dance is referenced in the lines "up / up / up", "down / down / down" and "knees spread wide". These lines can also be said to reference the slaves' journey. For example, "down" refers to them entering the ship, "up" refers to them leaving the ship on arriving at their destination and "knees spread wide" could be a reference to the ship's low ceilings and the harshness of conditions onboard. Similarly to *What Were They Like?*, the references to culture and people's lives are fairly sad and negative. Instead of celebrating the culture, both poems mainly grieve over the loss of culture.

• The limbo dance and the music of the "drummers" seem to keep the spirits of the slaves up. The poet says "the music is saving me" and "the drummers are praising me". The poet seems to be making a statement that no matter what conditions he has to face, the music and traditions of his culture will keep him positive. He celebrates the survival of the slaves. This poem ends on a more positive note than *What Were They Like?*, which ends with the sense that all is destroyed and lost for good.

12. For this question, you must compare cultural details in *Presents from my Aunts…* with <u>one</u> other poem from the anthology. *What Were They Like?, Search For My Tongue, Not my Business, Two Scavengers…, Nothing's Changed, Limbo, Night of the Scorpion* and *Hurricane Hits England* all contain cultural details. I've picked *Two Scavengers…*. You only have 45 minutes to answer the question so just include a short introduction and conclusion and concentrate on comparing the poems. The most important thing to remember is to compare the poems. Don't just talk about one poem and then the other — you have to say how they're similar and different. Here are some points you could include in your answer:

• *Presents from my Aunts…* is a poem about a girl who is half English and half Pakistani. She receives presents from Pakistan which cause her to ponder her own identity. There are references in this poem to aspects of both Pakistani and British culture.

• The main references to Pakistani culture are the descriptions of clothes, such as "a salwar kameez", "embossed slippers", "Candy-striped glass bangles" and "an apple-green sari". The poet comments that she "could never be as lovely / as those clothes". She finds them beautiful, but also "alien" — they make her feel uncomfortable with herself.

• The poet mentions the war when East Pakistan became Bangladesh. She says, "there was conflict, a fractured land", and she compares this "conflict" to her own conflict of identity.

• The poet also mentions negative aspects of Pakistan such as "beggars", "sweeper-girls" and her aunts "screened from male visitors".

• There are also references to British culture in terms of clothes. She "longed for denim and corduroy" because she feels more comfortable in such plain and ordinary British clothes. She also says that her "aunts requested cardigans / from Marks and Spencers". There is humour and irony in this statement. Despite all the beautiful clothes they offer, the aunts too long for plain British clothes.

• *Two Scavengers…* also contains strong references to culture. It is a poem about two garbagemen and two rich people in a Mercedes who meet briefly at a stoplight. The garbagemen stare down at the couple, who don't seem to notice them. The poet uses this scenario to make a point about the huge gap that still exists between rich and poor in modern American society.

• The poem contains many references to details that are specific to American culture. For example, "a bright yellow garbage truck" will be a familiar sight to most Americans.

• Cultural references are used to emphasise the difference between the two types of people. For example, the garbagemen are in "red plastic blazers", while the rich man is "in a hip three-piece linen suit". Both men have long hair and sunglasses, but the garbagemen, in comparison to the "elegant couple" are "grungy from their route". As in *Presents from my Aunts…*, clothes are used to emphasise cultural differences.

• The poet refers to the older garbageman as "some gargoyle / Quasimodo", thus making reference to the hunchback from Victor Hugo's popular novel, which many Americans will be familiar with, especially from its numerous film adaptations. There is humour in this reference to popular culture, just as there is humour in the reference to "Marks and Spencers" in *Presents from my Aunts…*.

13. For this question you need to compare how description is used in *Night of the Scorpion* and <u>one</u> other poem from the anthology. *Island Man, Two Scavengers..., Nothing's Changed, Presents from my Aunts..., Blessing* and *Vultures* all contain description. I've picked *Vultures*. You only have 45 minutes to answer this question so just include a short introduction and conclusion and concentrate on talking about the poems. The most important thing to remember is to compare the poems. Don't just talk about one and then the other — you have to say how they are similar and different. Here are some points you could include in your answer:

• In *Night of the Scorpion,* the poet uses description to make the villagers seem panicked and illogical by describing them as "like swarms of flies."

• He describes the scorpion as the devil, "Evil One" and "diabolic"; this provides an effective comparison with the religious responses of the villagers.

• The description of the rites of the villagers is very detailed, for example: "May the sins of your previous birth / be burned away tonight." The repetition of "May" also makes the villagers' reactions seem like an instinctive response, rather than a helpful one.

• The poet also uses shocking images such as "my mother twisted through and through, / groaning on a mat." The mother's pain had almost been lost in the descriptions of the villagers' actions but this image brings the mother to the forefront. It also shows that the actions of the villagers are not helping ease the mother's pain.

• In *Vultures* the poet also uses descriptions that create an atmosphere of evil — it is grey and gloomy when the vultures appear: "In the greyness / and drizzle of one despondent / dawn." This can be compared to the "dark room" filled with "giant scorpion shadows" in *Night of the Scorpion*.

• The vultures' eyes are also described as "cold" and their eating habits are repulsive. This creates another link between the vultures and evil.

• The Commandant of Belsen is described in a similar way to the vultures. He is described as having "human roast clinging / rebelliously to his hairy / nostrils". This associates him with the vultures and the dead body in the trench.

• The poet also uses description to explain the central point of the poem. He describes love as a person who sleeps in a "charnel-house" instead of facing evil. This is the central problem of the poem; it is quite bleak to think that love cannot overcome evil. Yet the poet also argues that it could be positive that love can exist in evil places.

14. For this question you need to compare how description is used in *Presents from my Aunts in Pakistan* and <u>one</u> other poem from the anthology. *Nothing's Changed, Island Man, Night of the Scorpion, Two Scavengers..., Blessing* and *Vultures* all contain description. I've picked *Nothing's Changed*. You only have 45 minutes to answer this question so just include a short introduction and conclusion and concentrate on talking about the poems. The most important thing to remember is to compare the poems. Don't just talk about one and then the other — you have to say how they are similar and different. Here are some points you could include in your answer:

• The poet uses descriptions of the presents to show her mixed feelings. The presents are described as "lovely" but they are also "broad and stiff." This gives the impression they are not comfortable to wear.

• The poet also uses similes, for example "glistening like an orange split open". This shows that the clothes are exotic rather than normal to her. She prefers the "denim and corduroy" of Western clothes, but admires the beauty of her presents.

• The poet describes Pakistan as "fractured" — this could also refer to her own fractured identity.

• The poet compares herself to a phoenix who can't "rise up out" of the brightly coloured clothes she wears. She can't recreate herself and assume a Pakistani identity.

• The poet also tries to describe Pakistan but she can only imagine it through what she reads. This is a contrast to *Nothing's Changed* where the description of District Six is very vivid.

• In *Nothing's Changed* the poet uses description to demonstrate his feelings. He describes himself as "boy again, / leaving small mean O" showing that he is resentful of the "whites only inn."

• In *Nothing's Changed* the poet vividly describes the ground of District Six. It is full of weeds and cans, showing that it is run down compared to the inn, which has "linen falls" on the tables. In *Presents from my Aunts in Pakistan* the poet also describes the poverty and problems Pakistan has. This shows that inequality is present in both South Africa and Pakistan.

• The "whites only inn" is also described as squatting on the landscape. This is an ugly description and gives the impression that it doesn't belong there.

• The inn's name "flaring like a flag" gives the impression that it is taunting the poet, making him angry.

THE ANSWERS

15. For this question you need to compare how metaphors are used in *Vultures* and <u>one</u> other poem from the anthology. *Limbo, Nothing's Changed, Love After Love, Blessing, Search For My Tongue, This Room* and *Half-Caste* all use metaphors. I've picked *Search For My Tongue*. You only have 45 minutes to answer this question so just include a short introduction and conclusion and concentrate on talking about the poems. The most important thing to remember is to compare the poems. Don't just talk about one and then the other — you have to say how they are similar and different. Here are some points you could include in your answer:
• In *Vultures* the poet uses a vulture acting "affectionately" towards its mate as a metaphor for a Nazi officer who loves his children. The poet also writes that love is a woman who picks "a corner / in that charnel-house" and sleeps there, but has "her face / turned to the wall!" The poet argues that this is what is happening with the Commandant — he loves his children, but is blind to the suffering he inflicts on the Jews.
• The comparison between the Nazi officer and the vulture is powerful because the metaphors continually refer to each other — for example, the vultures are associated with death because they feed on a dead body. The Nazi officer is also associated with death and this strengthens the similarities between the two.
• The poet isn't sure whether the fact that the Nazi officer is loving towards his children is a positive thing or not — it could either make you "praise" or "despair" for society. It seems that love cannot conquer the evil. The Nazi officer does not show the Jews the same kindness he shows towards his children when he buys "chocolate / for his tender offspring".
• *Search For My Tongue* also uses lots of metaphors to strengthen the images it creates. The poet sees her mother tongue as a plant that "blossoms out of my mouth" and as a literal tongue that represents her second language: "what would you do / if you had two tongues in your mouth".
• As in *Vultures* the poet develops metaphors throughout the poem to make them stronger, for example when the poet describes how her mother tongue "grows longer, grows moist, grows strong veins" it is no longer a language, but an actual flower that blossoms and pushes the other tongue aside, which completes the comparison between the tongue and the plant.
• In contrast, the metaphors used in *Search For My Tongue* are more beautiful than that of *Vultures*. The image of a flower that "blossoms out of my mouth" is very attractive.

16. For this question you need to compare how metaphors are used in *Half-Caste* and <u>one</u> other poem from the anthology. *Limbo, Nothing's Changed, Love After Love, Blessing, Vultures, Search For My Tongue* and *This Room* all use metaphors. I've picked *Blessing*. You only have 45 minutes to answer this question so just include a short introduction and conclusion and concentrate on talking about the poems. The most important thing to remember is to compare the poems. Don't just talk about one and then the other — you have to say how they are similar and different. Here are some points you could include in your answer:
• In *Half-Caste* the poet compares being mixed race to other mixes, e.g. Picasso's paintings or the weather. This reinforces the message that being called "half-caste" is an insult to something both beautiful and natural.
• The use of metaphors shows how nonsensical the term "half-caste" is as we don't call other things that are mixes, e.g. a "symphony", half-caste.
• The poet's use of humorous metaphors also helps to reinforce the message, e.g. the poet goes on to compare being called "half-caste" to the English weather: "england weather / nearly always half-caste / in fact some o dem cloud / half-caste till dem overcast." The poet's use of humour is particularly effective when the poet goes on to say "ah rass" (an expression of disgust) which really makes the reader take notice of what the poet is saying.
•In *Blessing,* the poet does not use humour to reinforce her message — Dharker uses religious imagery instead. The poet describes water as the "voice of a kindly god", which makes the water seem more valuable. This reinforces how important the water is to them.
•The poet uses the theme of religion as an extended metaphor when she describes the villagers as a "congregation". In "Half-Caste" the poet also uses an extended metaphor when he claims he is "lookin at yu wid de keen / half of mih eye." He uses the idea of becoming half a person when he is called "half-caste" to demonstrate how demeaning it is, and it also has a comic effect.
•Further on in "Blessing" the poet also uses imagery of light to describe the children dancing in the water, e.g. "flashing light." This reinforces how joyful and miraculous the water is. This could make the reader think about their own response to water, and the fact that they take for granted what is so highly prized in another country.

17. For this question you need to compare how unusual presentation is used in *Unrelated Incidents* and <u>one</u> other poem from the anthology. *Two Scavengers..., Presents from my Aunts..., What Were They Like?, Limbo* and *Search For My Tongue* all use unusual presentation. I've picked *Limbo*. You only have 45 minutes to answer this question so just include a short introduction and conclusion and concentrate on talking about the poems. The most important thing to remember is to compare the poems. Don't just talk about one and then the other — you have to say how they are similar and different. Here are some points you could include in your answer:
   • In *Unrelated Incidents* the poem is set out like an autocue, and this reflects the poet's negative views on the news always being read out by people who use perfectly spoken 'standard' English.
   • The layout also adds to the idea that the poet is presenting his views as the "trooth", as if it was really on the news.
   • The spelling the poet uses also adds to the effect, as it makes his accent come through more strongly. You hear his true voice in the poem and this gives the impression that the poet won't be forced into standard English just because it is respected more than regional accents.
   • The short sentences seem more abrupt — this has the effect of making the poet seem angrier. This reflects his disgust that regional accents are distrusted and seen as 'common'.
   • In *Limbo* the poet also uses abrupt, short lines similar to *Unrelated Incidents*. For example the layout of "down / down / down" reads like a descent. This shows the poet's descent into slavery, and how his value as a human being is lowered.
   • The short lines also give the poem a harsh beat, much like that of a drum. This, along with the spaces between the lines, emphasises the fact that it's a rhythmic dance.
   • The fact that the poem is one long sentence emphasises the relentlessness of slave labour and the poet's anger at slavery. This is similar to how the poet expresses his anger in *Unrelated Incidents*.
   • The italics in *"limbo / limbo like me"* read like a chorus, which shows the rhythm of the dance that is in the background. This reinforces the poet's West Indian roots.

18. For this question you need to compare how unusual presentation is used in *What Were They Like?* and <u>one</u> other poem from the anthology. *Unrelated Incidents, Presents from my Aunts..., Two Scavengers in a Truck, Two Beautiful People in a Mercedes, Limbo* and *Search For My Tongue* all use unusual presentation. I've picked *Two Scavengers...* You only have 45 minutes to answer this question so just include a short introduction and conclusion and concentrate on talking about the poems. The most important thing to remember is to compare the poems. Don't just talk about one and then the other — you have to say how they are similar and different. Here are some points you could include in your answer:
   • *What Were They Like?* uses questions and answers, to make it look like a formal investigation. Each pair of questions covers a particular part of Vietnamese culture. This reinforces the poet's ideas that Vietnamese culture has been destroyed, and someone is trying to find out what has been lost.
   • The seriousness conveyed by the presentation contrasts with the poetic language used, e.g. "Were they inclined to quiet laughter?" This makes the Vietnamese culture seem even more fragile and beautiful by comparison.
   • The words used also change their meanings from question to answer, e.g. in question four "bone" is seen as something that the Vietnamese people would use to make ornaments, but bone represents "charred" human bodies in the answer. This shows the Vietnamese culture has been destroyed.
   • In *Two Scavengers*, the lines are indented, which emphasises the separation between the Mercedes and the garbage men, especially in the lines "and looking down into / an elegant open Mercedes."
   • The line separation gives emphasis to certain words: "looking down like some / gargoyle Quasimodo." This places more emphasis on "gargoyle Quasimodo" and the ugliness of the garbage men compared to the "cool couple"
   • On the last line the poet describes the "small gulf" between the Mercedes and the garbage men — the space between them at the traffic lights was small, but by using spaces between the lines the poet emphasises how big the gap really is.

19. For this question you need to compare how non-standard English is used and how it relates to culture in *Limbo* and one other poem from the anthology. *Island Man, Unrelated Incidents* and *Half-Caste* all use non-standard English. I've picked *Island Man*. You only have 45 minutes to answer this question so just include a short introduction and conclusion and concentrate on talking about the poems. The most important thing to remember is to compare the poems. Don't just talk about one and then the other — you have to say how they are similar and different. Here are some points you could include in your answer:

• The language used in Limbo reflects the slaves' culture because the poet writes in Creole. This helps the reader see the slaves' point of view. If the poet had just written in standard English it would not have had the same effect.

• Creole uses simplified grammar, which helps convey the cruelty of how the slaves were punished, e.g. "stick hit sound". The alliteration in this phrase also contributes to its harsh sound.

• As the poet doesn't use punctuation, the full stop at the end comes as a shock. It helps emphasise the end of the poem and the end of the dance, the poet's life and slavery.

• In *Island Man* the poet uses non-standard English to reflect the culture of the man in the poem. The poet uses the word "wombing" to give the impression that the man views the Caribbean as a place of safety. Using "wombing" with "breaking" also gives the impression of the sea going in and out, which is a soothing image.

• Like *Limbo*, *Island Man* lacks punctuation and this gives the poem a dreamy feel. The repetition of "groggily groggily" without a comma shows the man's difficulty in waking up in the morning, as it is harder for the reader to process.

• Using the word "sands" instead of "sounds" shows that the poet is still stuck between the two cultures of the Caribbean and London.

• *Island Man* deals with culture in a gentler way than *Limbo*; the Island Man sees the culture he has lost as something that comforts him and something he misses, which is a contrast to the horrors of slavery in *Limbo*.

20. For this question, you must compare the use of non-standard English in *Unrelated Incidents* with <u>one</u> other poem from the anthology. *Island Man, Half-Caste* and *Limbo* are the poems which contain the best examples of non-standard English. I've picked *Half-Caste*. You only have 45 minutes to answer the question so just include a short introduction and conclusion and concentrate on comparing the poems. The most important thing to remember is to compare the poems. Don't just talk about one poem and then the other — you have to say how they're similar and different. Here are some points you could include in your answer:

• In *Unrelated Incidents*, the poet spells words phonetically to make them sound like a strong Glaswegian accent when read out loud. For example, he writes "widny wahnt" for "wouldn't want". This is ironic because the poem is about a newsreader explaining that if he spoke with a regional accent, people wouldn't trust him.

• The newsreader insults (in a regional accent) the very people who would have that accent — he calls working-class people "yoo scruff". This ironic use of non-standard English is extremely effective and delivers a powerful message.

• The poem starts without capital letters or speech marks. This has two effects — it makes it informal, like someone's talking, and it shows that the poet won't be forced into using standard English.

• There is irony in the misspelling of "spellin" and the phrase "thirza right / way ti spell / ana right way / ti tok it".

• The poet changes from the Glaswegian accent into a 'posh' newsreader's accent at the end in the word "nyooz". It is comical and mocks the 'posh' newsreader and his opinions about the right way to talk.

• In *Half-Caste*, the poet also uses non-standard English. As in *Unrelated Incidents*, he spells some words phonetically, which in this poem makes them sound like they're spoken with a Caribbean accent when read aloud.

• The poet uses non-standard English to sound chatty and conversational, such as in "well in dat case". He also uses it to sound confrontational, such as in "Explain yuself", in order to express his anger at the idea of mixed-race people being 'incomplete'. He even uses it to express his disgust at this idea, such as with the expression "ah rass".

• As in *Unrelated Incidents*, non-standard punctuation is used for effect. In *Half-Caste*, there is no standard punctuation at all and very few capital letters. The effect of this is that the poem sounds direct and informal. As with *Unrelated Incidents*, it also expresses the feeling that the poet is comfortable with his identity — he doesn't feel the need to conform to standard punctuation. He also deliberately omits capital letters from names, such as "picasso", which could be to make a statement about everyone being equal.

• The poet mixes Caribbean Creole with standard English, such as "some o dem cloud" mixed with "in fact". Through this technique, the poet shows that he's comfortable with his mixed background.

• In both poems, the use of non-standard English creates a humorous effect. In Half-Caste, "england weather / nearly always half-caste" is a funny idea which shows how silly the term 'half-caste' is, and how completely natural it is to be mixed race. The humour in both poems helps the poets to get their messages across. For example, the phrase "why I offer yu half-a-hand" creates a nonsensical image which shows how ridiculous the idea of being half a person really is.

21. For this question you need to compare how a strong sense of place is created in *Nothing's Changed* and <u>one</u> other poem. *Island Man, Blessing, Two Scavengers..., What Were They Like?, Presents from my Aunts..., Hurricane Hits England* and *Vultures* are all about particular places. I've picked *Vultures*. You only have 45 minutes to answer this question, so just include a short introduction and conclusion and concentrate on talking about the poems. The most important thing to remember is to compare the poems. Don't just talk about one and then the other — you have to say how they are similar and different. Here are some points you could include in your answer:

• In *Nothing's Changed,* the detailed descriptions of the ground in District Six make the reader feel like they are standing in the poet's shoes, and make the poet sound like he knows the area well.

• The poet also instinctively knows where he is "my feet know, / and my hands" adding to the impression that the poet's whole body recognises the area.

• The separation in District Six represents the whole of South Africa. There is a clear difference between the "new, up-market" white inn and the "working man's cafe", which shows that there is still apartheid 'of a sort' in South Africa.

• The fact that the poet writes "we know where we belong" shows that the divisions between black and white South Africans are still pronounced.

• In *Vultures* the poet also uses detailed imagery to give a strong sense of place, just like in *Nothing's Changed*. The poet does this by using descriptions that give an impression of death and greyness to the scene, for example: "In the greyness / and drizzle of one despondent / dawn".

• The poet also creates an atmosphere of death by using images of "broken / bone of a dead tree" and the "swollen / corpse" in the trench. This strengthens the link between vultures and death, and provides an effective contrast to the love between the vultures.

• Using imagery of death and evil provides an effective background for the evil of the Commandant. This is different from *Nothing's Changed,* as Afrika concentrates on using contrasting images to show the difference between the black and white areas, whereas Achebe uses imagery of death to create similarities between the vultures and the Commandant.

22. For this question you need to compare how the description of places is used to create a sense of different cultures in *Hurricane Hits England* and <u>one</u> other poem. *Island Man, Blessing, What Were They Like?, Presents from my Aunts..., Two Scavengers..., Nothing's Changed* and *Vultures* are all about particular places. I've picked *Presents from my Aunts in Pakistan*. You only have 45 minutes to answer this question so just include a short introduction and conclusion and concentrate on talking about the poems. The most important thing to remember is to compare the poems. Don't just talk about one and then the other — you have to say how they are similar and different. Here are some points you could include in your answer:

• In *Hurricane Hits England* the poet describes a hurricane in England and how it makes her feel more closely connected to the English landscape.

• The description of the wind as Caribbean and African weather gods, for example "Huracan" and "Oya" makes the storm seem more powerful and more meaningful to the poet, as it reminds her of her Caribbean roots.

• The poet further describes their "rage", showing how the gods were responsible for changes in the weather.

• The image of the trees falling "heavy as whales" also links England with the Caribbean sea.

• In *Presents from my Aunts in Pakistan* the poet uses descriptions of Pakistan to give her an idea of the culture; she has to imagine most of it and is confused about her attachment to Pakistan.

• The conflict between cultures is present in both of the poems, but in *Hurricane Hits England* the poet resolves the conflict by realising that it does not matter where you live. Contrastingly in *Presents from my Aunts in Pakistan* the poet still does not feel wholly English or Pakistani.

• The phrase "fractured land" gives the impression that the poet can't quite remember Pakistan and has problems identifying with it, but also the conflict within Pakistan. This contrasts with Nichols, who has a strong connection to her Caribbean roots — she aligns herself to the "movement" of the Caribbean winds.

• The reference to "beggars, sweeper-girls" also gives the impression that Pakistan has problems with poverty.

• The poet describes the fashions of Pakistan in a beautiful way, e.g. "apple-green sari", which gives an indication of the culture and how different the mode of dress is from English fashion.

23. For this question you need to compare how two cultures are used in *Island Man* and <u>one</u> other poem. *Hurricane Hits England, Presents from my Aunts in Pakistan, Unrelated Incidents, Half-Caste* and *Search For My Tongue* are all about two contrasting cultures. I've picked *Search for my Tongue*. You only have 45 minutes to answer this question so just include a short introduction and conclusion and concentrate on talking about the poems. The most important thing to remember is to compare the poems. Don't just talk about one and then the other — you have to say how they are similar and different. Here are some points you could include in your answer:

• In *Island Man* the contrast between London and the Caribbean gives the impression that the man is unhappy in his home and longs for the Caribbean. The "dull North Circular roar" of London is compared to the Caribbean sea.

• The imagery surrounding London seems grey, depressing and relentless compared to the beautiful imagery surrounding the Caribbean, e.g. "small emerald island".

• The effort the man goes through to get himself up for work is physical; he has to heave himself up and muffle his thoughts of home in the Caribbean. This contrasts to the ease with which he describes his Caribbean life: "wild seabirds / and fisherman pushing out to sea".

• *Search For My Tongue* is another poem that shows conflicting cultures. The poet feels like she is losing her "mother tongue" and misses it; much as the persona in *Island Man* misses the Caribbean.

• The contrast between the two cultures is made even more effective by using the Gujarati script as a visual contrast in the poem. *Island Man* also uses structural devices to create contrast between the two cultures, e.g. indenting "surge of wheels" shows that "surge" could relate to the sea but "wheels" relates to London. It makes it stand out from the rest of the poem and shows that the island man feels lost between London and Caribbean culture.

• The poet in *Search For My Tongue* shows contrast and conflict as well, as the two tongues cannot be used "both together", but if she neglects her mother tongue she is frightened of losing it.

• The poet seems to prefer her Gujarati language to English, as her mother tongue "ties the other tongue in knots", showing that to her it is more powerful than English. It may be closer to her heart too.

24. For this question you need to compare how conflicting cultures are portrayed in *Presents from my Aunts in Pakistan* and <u>one</u> other poem from the anthology. *Hurricane Hits England, Unrelated Incidents, Search For My Tongue* and *Island Man* are all poems with two conflicting cultures. I've picked *Unrelated Incidents*. You only have 45 minutes to answer this question so just include a short introduction and conclusion and concentrate on talking about the poems. The most important thing to remember is to compare the poems. Don't just talk about one and then the other — you have to say how they are similar and different. Here are some points you could include in your answer:

• In *Presents from my Aunts in Pakistan* the poet feels like an outsider both in England and Pakistan because she feels the two cultures clash. The poet shows the contrast by discussing what she feels like when she wears her Pakistani clothes, e.g. she feels "alien in the sitting-room".

• The poet also uses clothes to show the difference between Western society and Pakistani culture. Her friend does not like her "salwar kameez" and the bright colours of her Pakistani clothes seem to clash with her Western clothes.

• English and Pakistani cultures also clash when her mother's jewellery is stolen from her car — this could be symbolic of England stealing her Pakistani identity.

• She feels as if she has "no fixed nationality" and she can only look through the "fretwork / at the Shalimar Gardens". This creates the image that there is a barrier between her and her Pakistani identity.

• In *Unrelated Incidents* the poet rejects the 'posh' English culture, whereas, in *Presents from my Aunts in Pakistan,* the poet tries to reconcile the two cultures.

• The poet in *Unrelated Incidents* seems to have a more definite identity compared to the poet in *Presents from my Aunts in Pakistan;* he rejects standard pronunciation and grammar to demonstrate his Scottish roots.

• He mocks the attitude that regional accents are seen as untrustworthy and common: "if / a toktaboot / thi trooth / lik wanna yoo / scruff yi / widny thingk / it wuz troo" compared to the "BBC accent" that has a higher status.

• The structure of the poem is like an autocue, which highlights the difference between the BBC accent and the regional accent — you wouldn't see this kind of language on an autocue.

25. For this question you need to compare how universal ideas are presented in *Hurricane Hits England* and <u>one</u> other poem from the anthology. *Nothing's Changed, Vultures, This Room, Two Scavengers..., Love After Love* and *Half-Caste* are all poems that feature universal ideas. I've picked *Love After Love*. You only have 45 minutes to answer this question so just include a short introduction and conclusion and concentrate on talking about the poems. The most important thing to remember is to compare the poems. Don't just talk about one and then the other — you have to say how they are similar and different. Here are some points you could include in your answer:
- In *Hurricane Hits England* the poet explores feeling out of place, but by the end of the poem she feels more connected to England.
- She presents this theme by seeing the hurricane in England as storm gods from the Caribbean and Africa; she tries to communicate with them — "Talk to me Huracan" — as these types of storms would be familiar to her.
- The storm has a great effect on her; she describes it as a "blinding illumination", referring both to the lightning and the enlightenment she experiences because of the storm.
- She asks the storm to "Come to break the frozen lake in me", showing that she had been unable to connect with the landscape before the storm took place.
- She realises that "the earth is the earth is the earth" and that all places are connected; she no longer feels distanced from the Caribbean or England.
- *Love After Love* also explores the universal idea of identity, much like *Hurricane Hits England*. In this poem the poet explores the idea of finding happiness within yourself, similar to the way Nichols has a "blinding illumination" within herself that enables her to connect with the landscape.
- Like *Hurricane Hits England* it discusses universal feelings we can all relate to and ends on a positive note; "Feast on your life" implies that we should enjoy our lives, and especially if we are single.
- The poet explores the idea that we often become someone else when we are in a relationship; he says to ex-lovers, "Give back your heart / To itself" meaning that they will get to know themselves again. He uses the idea of a meal as a celebration, showing that being on your own can be a positive thing.

26. For this question you need to compare how the universal idea of good and evil is presented in *Vultures* and <u>one</u> other poem from the anthology. *Nothing's Changed, Half-Caste, This Room, Hurricane Hits England, Two Scavengers..., Love After Love* and *Not my Business* are all poems that feature universal ideas. I've picked *Not my Business*. You only have 45 minutes to answer this question so just include a short introduction and conclusion and concentrate on talking about the poems. The most important thing to remember is to compare the poems. Don't just talk about one and then the other — you have to say how they are similar and different. Here are some points you could include in your answer:
- In *Vultures* the poet uses the specific examples of vultures and a concentration camp "Commandant" to explore the idea that good and evil can exist in the same person. The vultures are creatures associated with evil, and they feed on dead bodies, but the vulture is also seen inclining "affectionately" towards its mate.
- The poet contemplates the vultures and discusses that love "will pick a corner / in that charnel-house / tidy it and coil up there". This shows that love can be found in the most unlikely places, but also that love cannot conquer evil. The poet thinks that it is "Strange" rather than tragic, and leaves the reader to make up their own mind.
- By using the examples of the vultures and the Commandant he shows that this contrast between good and evil can be everywhere.
- The poet also discusses that it could be positive that even in an "ogre / a tiny glow-worm / tenderness" can be found, but also negative because love will always be infected with evil.
- In *Not my Business* the poet also deals with a specific situation and applies it to life in general. The poet describes what it's like living under a brutal regime and what happens when you don't face up to what's going on.
- Like in *Vultures* the tone is mainly unemotional, describing gruesome occurrences in a matter-of-fact way: "They picked Akanni up one morning / Beat him soft like clay."
- The shock comes at the end of the poem, when the poet realises they have come for him: "The jeep was waiting on my bewildered lawn / Waiting, waiting in its usual silence." This shows that you can't ignore what is happening to your friends just because it doesn't affect you, as the likelihood is that it will eventually. The poem encourages people to speak up against this type of regime.

27. For this question you need to compare the themes of tradition in *Night of the Scorpion* and <u>one</u> other poem in the anthology. *What Were They Like?, Presents from my Aunts in Pakistan, Limbo* and *Hurricane Hits England* are all poems that feature traditions. I've picked *What Were They Like?* You only have 45 minutes to answer this question so just include a short introduction and conclusion and concentrate on talking about the poems. The most important thing to remember is to compare the poems. Don't just talk about one and then the other — you have to say how they are similar and different. Here are some points you could include in your answer:

   • In *Night of the Scorpion* the poet could be seen as critical of the way the villagers try to help his mother by using religion. Chanting "the name of God a hundred times" does not help them find the scorpion in the end, showing that the religious beliefs don't help them in this particular case.
   • The villagers also seem unhelpful when they talk about his mother's next life: "May the sins of your previous birth / be burned away tonight". They have already decided that she is going to die.
   • The holy man's actions also don't seem practical; they have a ceremonial feel. He tries to tame the poison with an "incantation".
   • At the end, "After twenty hours / it lost its sting" — the matter-of-fact tone used shows that this was the inevitable outcome — there was no need for the villagers to panic.
   • *What Were They Like?* describes traditions that have been lost, much like the outdated traditions described in *Night of the Scorpion.*
   • In contrast, the traditions described in *What Were They Like?* seem calm and beautiful, e.g. "stone lanterns illumined pleasant ways", unlike the traditions described in *Night of the Scorpion*, which are criticised by the poet.
   • The poet also uses examples to suggest that the Vietnamese culture had things in common with ours, like ceremonies and ornaments.
   • The poem is also written in the present tense, for example "It is not remembered", demonstrating how much has been lost. This is in contrast to *Night of the Scorpion,* which opens in present tense "I remember" and then continues in past tense for the rest of the poem.

28. For this question you need to compare how traditions are referred to in *Presents from my Aunts in Pakistan* and <u>one</u> other poem in the anthology. *Night of the Scorpion, What Were They Like?, Limbo* and *Hurricane Hits England* are all poems that feature traditions. I've picked *Hurricane Hits England.* You only have 45 minutes to answer this question so just include a short introduction and conclusion and concentrate on talking about the poems. The most important thing to remember is to compare the poems. Don't just talk about one and then the other — you have to say how they are similar and different. Here are some points you could include in your answer:

   • In *Presents from my Aunts in Pakistan* the poet refers to traditional Pakistani clothes, for example a "salwar kameez", to demonstrate the differences between Pakistani and Western culture.
   • She feels "alien in the sitting-room", showing that she does not feel comfortable wearing Pakistani clothes in a Western environment; she feels more comfortable in "denim and corduroy".
   • The poet also uses a reference of "staring through the fretwork / at the Shalimar Gardens" to represent a barrier between the poet becoming wholly Pakistani or wholly English.
   • In *Hurricane Hits England* the poet uses traditional African and Mayan beliefs to help her relate to the landscape. As in *Presents from my Aunts in Pakistan*, she had been feeling out of place in England; "It took a hurricane, to bring her closer / To the landscape", but in *Hurricane Hits England* the poet seems to resolve her difficulties.
   • She refers to the hurricane as a "sweeping, back-home cousin" and by the names of the storm gods, showing that they remind her of home. The storm also reveals the author's cultural roots — "Shaking the foundations of the very trees within me" — and this shows that she becomes closer to her traditions and her culture.
   • It is because of the storm that she realises that "the earth is the earth is the earth" — she feels connected to both England and the Caribbean as a result.

**Glossary**

accent	The way people <u>pronouce words</u>. It can vary between different countries, regions and social backgrounds.
alliteration	Where consonant sounds are repeated. It's often used in poetry to give a nice pattern to a phrase. E.g. '<u>S</u>ally's <u>s</u>lipper <u>s</u>lipped on a <u>s</u>limy <u>s</u>lug.'
assonance	When words share the same vowel sound. E.g. "L<u>i</u>sa had a p<u>ie</u>ce of ch<u>ee</u>se before sh<u>e</u> went to sl<u>ee</u>p, to help her dr<u>ea</u>m."
consonant	All the letters in the alphabet that <u>aren't vowels</u>.
contrast	When two things are described in a way which emphasises <u>how different</u> they are. E.g. a poet might contrast two different places, or two different cultures.
dialect	<u>Regional variation</u> of a <u>language</u>. People from different places might use different words or different sentence constructions. E.g. in some northern English dialects, people might say "Ey up" instead of "Hello".
empathy	When someone feels like they <u>understand</u> what someone else is experiencing and how they <u>feel</u> about it.
imagery	Language that creates a <u>picture in your mind</u>, bringing the text to life.
language	The <u>choice of words</u> used. The language determines the effect the piece of writing will have on the reader, e.g. it can be emotive or persuasive.
layout	The way a piece of writing is visually <u>presented</u> to the reader. E.g. what kind of <u>font</u> is used, whether there are subheadings and bullet points, how the <u>verses</u> in a poem are broken up, whether sentences or lines are arranged regularly, whether they create some kind of visual pattern, etc.
metaphor	A way of describing something by saying that it <u>is something else</u>, to create a vivid image. E.g. "His eyes were deep, black, oily pools."
narrator	The <u>voice</u> speaking the words that you're reading. E.g. a poem could be written from the point of view of a young child, which means the young child is the poem's narrator.
non-standard English	Any form of English that isn't formal English. Things like <u>slang</u>, <u>phonetic spelling</u> and <u>dialect</u> are all examples of non-standard English.
onomatopoeia	When a word <u>sounds like</u> what it's supposed to mean. E.g. "buzz", "crunch", "bang", "pop", "ding".
personification	A special kind of metaphor where you write about something as if it's a <u>person</u> with thoughts and feelings. E.g. "The sea growled hungrily."

Glossary

phonetic spelling	When words are spelt as they <u>sound</u> rather than with their usual spelling. It's often used to show that someone's speaking with a certain <u>accent</u>.
pun	A "play on words" — a word or phrase that's deliberately used because it has <u>more than one meaning</u>. E.g. "She lies on the couch at the psychiatrist's", where "lies" could mean "lies down" or "tells lies".
repetition	Obvious really — where a word or phrase is <u>repeated</u> to emphasise a point or idea.
rhythm	When sentences or lines have a <u>regular pattern</u> of strong and weak syllables. It's often used in poetry.
simile	A way of describing something by <u>comparing</u> it to something else, usually by using the words "like" or "as". E.g. "He was as pale as the moon," or "Her hair was like a bird's nest."
stanza	A <u>group of lines</u> in a poem that usually share the same rhythm pattern and have similar line lengths. Stanzas can also be called <u>verses</u>.
stereotype	An inaccurate, <u>generalised</u> view of a particular <u>group of people</u>. E.g. a stereotype of football fans might be that they're all hooligans.
structure	How a piece of writing is <u>arranged</u>. E.g. how it begins, develops and ends, whether it uses verses or not, whether it has a particular layout, etc.
syllable	A single <u>unit of sound</u> within a word. E.g. "all" has one syllable, "always" has two and "establishmentarianist" has eight.
symbolism	When an object <u>stands for something else</u>. E.g. a candle might be a symbol of hope, or a dying flower could symbolise the end of a relationship.
theme	An <u>idea</u> or <u>topic</u> that's important in a piece of writing. E.g. a poem could be based on the theme of friendship.
tone	The <u>mood</u> of a piece of writing, e.g. happy, sad, serious, lighthearted. It's an overall effect, created by things like choice of words, imagery and layout.
voice	The <u>personality</u> narrating the poem. Many poems are written either using the poet's voice, as if they're speaking to you <u>directly</u>, or the voice of a <u>character</u>, e.g. an elderly man, or a horse.
vowel	Simple — the letters 'a', 'e', 'i', 'o' and 'u' and sometimes 'y'.

Index

Acknowledgements

The publisher would like to thank:

Chinua Achebe `Vultures' from *Collected Poems* published by Carcanet, reprinted by permission of David Higham Associates.

Tatamkhulu Afrika 'Nothing's Changed' from *Night Rider: Selected Poems*, published by Kwela Books.

John Agard `Half-Caste' copyright © 1996 by John Agard, reproduced by kind permission of John Agard c/o Caroline Sheldon Literary Agency Limited.

Moniza Alvi 'Presents from my Aunts in Pakistan' from *Carrying My Wife,* Bloodaxe Books, 2000.

Sujata Bhatt `Search For My Tongue' from *Brunizem* (1998), reprinted by permission of the publishers, Carcanet Press Ltd.

Edward Kamau Brathwaite 'Limbo' from *The Arrivants: A New World Trilogy* (OUP, 1973), reprinted by permission of Oxford University Press.

Imtiaz Dharker 'Blessing' from *Postcards from god,* Bloodaxe Books, 1997; 'This Room' from *I Speak for the Devil,* Bloodaxe Books, 2001.

Nissim Ezekiel 'Night of the Scorpion' from *Poverty Poems*, reproduced by permission of Oxford University Press India, New Delhi.

Lawrence Ferlinghetti `Two Scavengers in a Truck, Two Beautiful People in a Mercedes' by Lawrence Ferlinghetti, from THESE ARE MY RIVERS, copyright © 1979 by Lawrence Ferlinghetti. Reprinted by permission of New Directions Publishing Corp.

Tom Leonard `Unrelated Incidents' © Tom Leonard, from *Intimate Voices,* Etruscan Books, Devon.

Denise Levertov `What Were They Like?' from *Selected Poems,* Bloodaxe Books, 1986. Reproduced by permission of Pollinger Limited and the proprietor.

Grace Nichols `Hurricane Hits England' Copyright © Grace Nichols 1996 reproduced with permission of Curtis Brown Group Ltd; `Island Man' Copyright © Grace Nichols 1984 reproduced with permission of Curtis Brown Group Ltd.

Niyi Osundare `Not my Business' from *Songs of the Seasons* © Niyi Osundare (Heinemann Educational Books, Nigeria, 1990).

Derek Walcott 'Love after Love' from SEA GRAPES by Derek Walcott. Copyright © 1976 by Derek Walcott. Reprinted by permission of Farrar, Straus and Giroux, LLC.

Photographs:
Photograph of Edward Kamau Brathwaite Kamau Brathwaite as guest author at the 4th annual St. Martin Book Fair, 2006. (House of Nehesi Publishers photo, 2006).
Photograph of Grace Nichols © Sheila Geraghty, reprinted by permission of Penguin Books
Photograph of Tatamkhulu Afrika Picture by Martin Phillips / Devon Education Services
Photograph of Imtiaz Dharker © Simon Powell
Photograph of Lawrence Ferlinghetti © Abraham Aronow, courtesy of New Directions
Photograph of Chinua Achebe by AFP/Getty Images, © Getty Images
Photograph of Denise Levertov by David Geier, courtesy of New Directions
Photograph of Sujata Bhatt image is given with the consent of Carcanet Press
Photograph of Tom Leonard Photo: Gordon Wright
Photograph of John Agard © Sheila Geraghty, reprinted by permission of Penguin Books
Photograph of Derek Walcott by Horst Tappe, Hulton Archive, © Getty Images
Photograph of Niyi Osundare © Niyi Osundare
Photograph of Moniza Alvi © Bob Coe
`Plan of slaves crammed into one deck on a slaveship' from Hulton Archive, © Getty Images

Make sure you're not missing out on another superb CGP revision book that might just save your life...

...order your **free** catalogue today.

CGP customer service is second to none

We work very hard to despatch all orders the **same day** we receive them, and our success rate is currently 99.9%. We send all orders by **overnight courier** or **First Class** post.
If you ring us today you should get your catalogue or book tomorrow. Irresistible, surely?

- Phone: 0870 750 1252   (Mon-Fri, 8.30am to 5.30pm)
- Fax: 0870 750 1292
- e-mail: orders@cgpbooks.co.uk
- Post: CGP, Kirkby-in-Furness, Cumbria, LA17 7WZ
- Website: www.cgpbooks.co.uk

...or you can ask at any good bookshop.